# Fare for Friends

# Fare for Friends

**KEY PORTER** BOOKS

**Canadian Cataloguing in Publication Data**

Fare for friends / Fare for Friends Foundation.

ISBN 978-1-55470-237-4

1. Cookery.  I. Fare for Friends Foundation

TX714.F366 2009            641.5           C2009-901418-1

THE CANADA COUNCIL | LE CONSEIL DES ARTS
FOR THE ARTS | DU CANADA
SINCE 1957 | DEPUIS 1957

ONTARIO ARTS COUNCIL
CONSEIL DES ARTS DE L'ONTARIO

The publisher gratefully acknowledges the support of the Canada Council for
the Arts and the Ontario Arts Council for its publishing program.

Key Porter Books Limited
6 Adelaide Street East, 10th floor
Toronto, Ontario
M5C 1H6

www.keyporter.com

Design: Peter Maher
Electronic formatting: Heidi Palfrey

Originally published in 1983.

Printed and bound in Canada

09 10 11 12 13  6 5 4 3 2 1

Mixed Sources
Product group from well-managed
forests, controlled sources and
recycled wood or fiber
www.fsc.org  Cert no. SW-COC-002358
© 1996 Forest Stewardship Council
FSC

ANCIENT FOREST ™
FRIENDLY

# A Special Project

Each year, thousands of women and their children suffer serious physical and psychological abuse. These victims must have an avenue of escape and a haven of protection where they can remain safe until they regain their strength.

Interim Place, a shelter for abused women and their children, is one such haven. Located in Mississauga, Canada, it provides refuge and encourages women to rebuild their lives.

In 1983 *Fare for Friends* was created by a dedicated group of women as a fundraiser for Interim Place. It quickly became a Canadian bestseller. Encouraged by the success of this project, a second book, *Good Friends Cookbook*, was published in 1991. Proceeds from both these books assist Interim Place in specific and meaningful ways.

Interim Place II opened its doors in 1992, fulfilling an increased need in the community.

It is with tremendous satisfaction that this group of authors, along with the help of Key Porter Books, reissues this revised and updated *Fare for Friends*. We hope that you will continue to support our special project.

Judy Leach, Chair
Eleanor Ball
Gail Bascombe
Lyn Bolt
Jane Buckland
Doreen Burke
Joan Corbett
Libby Dal Bianco
Jenny Dale
Gail Fargey
Joyce George
Mary Gilpin
Ruth Kitchen
Sandy Langdale
Sue MacIntosh
Wilma Mason
Beth Miller
Ann Morin
Jennifer Porteous
Sue Rowland
Mary Toye
Doreen White
Silvia Wilson

# And Again, for You, the Book!!

Being an integral part of an incredibly successful project is an inspiring experience. More than twenty-five years ago, when we started down the *Fare for Friends* road, we had no idea that our involvement and commitment to this cause would span almost three decades, lead to a Canadian bestselling cookbook, then to a second bestseller, *Good Friends Cookbook*, and raise in the process hundreds of thousands of dollars for Interim Place. Never in our wildest dreams could we have imagined such success. We've never looked back.

*Fare for Friends* has been revised and given a new look. Where possible, suggestions, tips and alternatives have been included to suit our healthier lifestyles. All changes were throughly tested and in many cases actually improved the original recipes.

Good food that tastes good is still our number one priority, but making it healthier and less fattening is equally important. "All things in moderation" is always a good guide.

*Fare for Friends* continues to be a treasury of sumptuous recipes—our favourites, our friends' favourites, and our friends' friends' favourites. It is our hope that this book will become a treasury of your favourites as well.

We've tried to make the recipes simple and spectacular, unique and delectable. Above all, we've endeavoured to share with you the warm ambiance that cooking and eating good food with good friends brings.

For us, friendship was the glue that bound this whole project together. Good friends, good company, good food ... these are the legacies we pass to you.

# Contents

# Beginnings
## Hors d'oeuvres and Appetizers

# Cream Cheese Oyster Roll

*The flavour of this attractive appetizer actually improves if made 6-8 hours in advance.*

| | | | |
|---|---|---|---|
| 8 | ounces cream cheese, softened* | 250 | g |
| 1-1½ | tablespoons mayonnaise, regular or light | 15-25 | mL |
| ½-1 | teaspoon Worcestershire sauce | 2-5 | mL |
| 1 | garlic clove, minced | 1 | |
| 1 | green onion, very finely chopped | 1 | |
| 1 | can (3.6 oz/104 g) smoked oysters, drained | 1 | |
| ¼ | cup parsley, chopped | 50 | mL |
| ¼ | cup walnuts, chopped | 50 | mL |

Blend mayonnaise with cream cheese. Mix in Worcestershire sauce, garlic and onion. Spread on oiled wax paper, ½ inch (1 cm) thick and in a rectangular shape. Cool 2 hours in the refrigerator. Mash oysters with fork and spread them over the cheese, keeping ¼ inch (0.5 cm) away from edges. Roll as a jelly roll and chill until ready to serve. Coat outside of roll with parsley and nuts. Serve with party rye bread or crackers.

**Serves 8**

**\*TIP:** Do not use light tub-style cream cheese in this recipe.

# Eleanor's Egg Caviar

*An eye catcher with great taste!*

| 5-6 | eggs, hard cooked, cooled and chopped | 5-6 | |
| 1 | small onion, grated or chopped fine (or 3-4 green onions) | 1 | |
| | Mayonnaise, regular or light, to taste | | |
| | Salt and pepper to taste | | |
| ½ | teaspoon curry powder | 2 | mL |
| 8 | ounces regular or light cream cheese, room temperature | 250 | g |
| 1½ | tablespoons sour cream, regular or light | 25 | mL |
| 1 | tablespoon mayonnaise, regular or light | 15 | mL |
| 1 | bottle (2 oz/60 g) red or black caviar | 1 | |

This hors d'oeuvre is made in three layers and eliminates the hassle of serving caviar with all its accompaniments. It can be made a day in advance, with the exception of adding the caviar, which should be done just before serving. Combine eggs, onion, mayonnaise and seasonings as for egg salad. Spread first layer in flan dish or shallow serving dish. Whip cream cheese and add just enough sour cream so that mixture is the consistency of fluffy icing. Add 1 tablespoon (15 mL) mayonnaise. Spread over egg salad layer. Top with caviar and garnish with sprigs of parsley or watercress. Serve with rice crackers or pumpernickel.

**Serves 10-12**

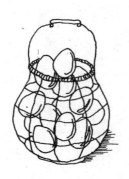

# Curried Mushroom Rolls

| 12-14 | thin slices bread | 12-14 | |
| | Soft butter | | |
| ¾ | pound fresh mushrooms, finely chopped | 375 | g |
| 2 | tablespoons melted butter | 30 | mL |
| ½ | teaspoon curry powder | 2 | mL |
| 1 | tablespoon lemon juice | 15 | mL |
| | Salt, pepper and cayenne to taste | | |
| | Additional melted butter | | |
| 1 | tablespoon flour if mixture is too runny | 15 | mL |

Preheat oven to 425°F (220°C). Remove the crusts from the bread and roll the slices to about ⅛ inch (3 mm) thick. Spread the surface of each slice thinly with butter and set aside. Sauté mushrooms until tender in melted butter. Add the spices and lemon juice. Spread about 1 tablespoon (15 mL) of mixture on each slice of bread. Roll like a jelly roll and cut into 3 pieces. Fasten each roll with a toothpick. Place on a baking sheet and lightly brush each roll with melted butter. Bake for about 10 minutes or until brown.

**Makes about 36 rolls**

# "Mary Vickers"

*A winner! People buy the book for this recipe!*

| 1 | loaf bread, thin sliced | 1 | |
| ½ | pound Cheddar cheese, shredded | 250 | g |
| 6 | slices bacon, fried crisp and crumbled | 6 | |
| 1 | 4 ounce package slivered almonds | 113 | g |
| 1 | onion, finely chopped | 1 | |
| 1 | cup mayonnaise, regular or light | 250 | mL |
| | Salt and pepper to taste | | |

Preheat oven to 400°F (200°C). Remove crusts from bread and spread each slice with a mixture of all other ingredients. Cut into strips or any desired shape. If desired, freeze on a baking sheet, place in plastic bags and store in freezer. To serve, bake for 10 minutes or until brown.
**Serves a crowd**

# Olive Cheese Melts

*This is a great make-ahead appetizer that freezes well.*

| | | |
|---|---|---|
| 1 | cup ripe olives, chopped | 250 mL |
| ⅓ | cup green onions, chopped | 75 mL |
| 1½ | cups old Cheddar cheese, grated | 375 mL |
| ½ | teaspoon curry powder | 2 mL |
| ½ | teaspoon salt | 2 mL |
| ½ | cup mayonnaise, regular or light | 125 mL |
| 8 | English muffins, halved | 8 |

Preheat oven to 400°F (200°C). Combine olives, green onions, cheese, curry powder, salt and mayonnaise. Spread on muffins and cut into 4 pieces. Can be frozen on cookie sheet at this point and put into freezer bags. Bake for 10 minutes.

**Makes 64**

# Marinated Fresh Mushrooms

mushrooms to fill a 1 quart (1 L) sealer jar

### MARINADE

| | | | |
|---|---|---|---|
| ⅔ | cup vegetable oil | 150 | mL |
| ⅓ | cup white vinegar | 75 | mL |
| | Salt and pepper to taste | | |
| ¼ | teaspoon paprika | 1 | mL |
| 1 | garlic clove, crushed* | 1 | |
| | Chives or green onions, chopped | | |

Wash and dry mushrooms. Cut large ones into quarters, leaving others whole. Place in jar. Pour marinade over top and seal. Refrigerate. Turn jar every so often. Best served after 3 or 4 days. Will keep in refrigerator for 7-10 days.

**\*TIP:** For more flavour increase garlic and add sprigs of rosemary and thyme.

# Sublime Asparagus Rolls

*These really are sublime!*

| | | | |
|---|---|---|---|
| 1 | bunch fresh asparagus, blanched and drained on paper towels (or 2 cans [each 10 oz/284 mL] asparagus) | 1 | |
| 2 | regular loaves sliced bread | 2 | |
| 8 | ounces blue cheese* | 250 | g |
| 8 | ounces cream cheese, regular or light | 250 | g |
| 1 | tablespoon mayonnaise, regular or light | 15 | mL |
| 1 | egg (optional) | 1 | |
| | Butter, melted | | |

Preheat oven to 350°F (180°C). Cut all crusts off bread and roll each slice flat with a rolling pin. Mix the cheeses, mayonnaise (and egg) in blender and spread onto bread. Top with one stalk of asparagus and roll up; cut into three pieces. Brush with melted butter and place on ungreased cookie sheet. These can be made the day before or frozen at this point. When ready to serve, bake for about 15 minutes, or until well browned.

**Makes 11 dozen**

**\*TIP:** Roquefort, Stilton, Cambozola, Gorgonzola cheeses can be used.

# Miniature Phyllo Cheese Bites

*A delicious hors d'oeuvre which can be made ahead and frozen!*

| | | | |
|---|---|---|---|
| ½ | pound frozen phyllo dough leaves, thawed | 250 | g |
| ½-¾ | cup unsalted butter, melted | 125-175 | mL |
| 8 | ounces cream cheese, softened | 250 | g |
| 8 | ounces Feta or chèvre cheese | 250 | g |
| ¼ | cup Parmesan cheese, grated | 50 | mL |
| 1 | cup parsley, chopped | 250 | mL |
| 1 | egg | 1 | |
| 2 | tablespoons fresh dill, chopped | 30 | mL |

Preheat oven to 350°F (180°C). Cut phyllo sheets into 4" × 8"
(10 cm × 20 cm) sections. Cover phyllo sheets first with a dry tea
towel and then a barely damp towel on top to prevent drying out.
Make cheese filling by mixing until smooth the cheeses, egg, parsley
and dill. Place one layer of phyllo on a clean surface; brush with
butter. Place ¾ teaspoon (4 mL) cheese filling in the centre at the
narrow end of phyllo piece. Fold each long side ½ inch (1 cm) toward
centre. Roll up tightly, beginning at narrow end, to make a little
enclosed tube. Place seam side down on well-buttered jelly roll pan.
Repeat with remaining phyllo pieces. Brush tops with butter. Bake
until pastries are golden, about 25 minutes. Pastries can also be
wrapped and frozen before baking for quick hors d'oeuvres.
**Makes 8-10 dozen**

# Cheese Puffs

*Keep a supply in your freezer.*

| | | |
|---|---|---|
| 1 | loaf Italian bread, unsliced | 1 |
| ½ | cup butter, softened | 125 mL |
| ⅓ | cup Mozzarella cheese, shredded | 75 mL |
| ⅓ | cup sharp Cheddar cheese, shredded | 75 mL |
| ⅓ | cup Swiss cheese, shredded | 75 mL |
| 4 | ounces cream cheese | 125 g |
| ½ | teaspoon dry mustard | 2 mL |
| ¼ | teaspoon cayenne pepper | 1 mL |
| | Salt to taste | |
| 2 | egg whites | 2 |

Trim crust from the entire loaf of bread. Cut bread into 1-inch (2.5-cm) cubes and set aside. In a saucepan, combine butter and all cheeses. Stir over moderate heat until well blended (or use microwave). Add mustard, cayenne and salt. Beat egg whites until stiff and fold into cheese mixture. Dip bread cubes into mixture one at a time, making sure each is well coated. Arrange on a baking sheet, making sure they don't touch. **Freeze.*** Remove from sheet and store in freezer until ready to use. Bake on ungreased sheet at 400°F (200°C) for approximately 10 minutes or until lightly browned.

**Serves a crowd**

**\*TIP:** If cheese puffs are not frozen first, bake at 325°F (160°C) until lightly browned.

# Spinach Cheese Cocktail Bites

*A versatile party hors d'oeuvre.*

| | | | |
|---|---|---|---|
| 3 | eggs | 3 | |
| 1 | cup flour | 250 | mL |
| 1 | cup milk | 250 | mL |
| 1 | teaspoon salt | 5 | mL |
| 1 | teaspoon baking powder | 5 | mL |
| 1 | tablespoon Dijon mustard | 15 | mL |
| | Dash of cayenne pepper | | |
| ¼ | cup chives, chopped | 50 | mL |
| 1 | pound Edam cheese, grated | 500 | g |
| 2 | packages (each 12 oz/340 g) frozen | 2 | |
| | chopped spinach, thawed and well drained | | |

Preheat oven to 350°F (180°C). Grease a 9" × 13" (3.5 L) cakepan well. In a large mixing bowl, beat eggs; add flour, milk, baking powder, salt, mustard, cayenne and chives. Blend well. Fold in cheese and spinach. Pour into pan and bake for 35 minutes or until almost set in centre. Allow to sit for about 15 minutes; cut into bite-sized squares and serve warm. These may also be frozen after baking and reheated in a 350°F (180°C) oven for 15-20 minutes at serving time.
**Makes about 10 dozen**

# Suzanne's Marinated Chinese Pork Tenderloin

*Succulent—an all-time winner as an hors d'oeuvre or an entrée!*

| | | | |
|---|---|---|---|
| 4 | green onions, sliced | 4 | |
| 4 | large garlic cloves, minced | 4 | |
| 2 | ounces fresh ginger, grated | 50 | g |
| 2 | tablespoons sugar | 30 | mL |
| ¼ | cup dry sherry | 50 | mL |
| ½ | cup soy sauce | 125 | mL |
| 2 | teaspoons Chinese Five Spice Powder, available at health food and oriental grocery stores | 10 | mL |
| 3 | whole pork tenderloins | 3 | |
| 1 | cup chutney or | 250 | mL |
| ½ | cup hot mustard | 125 | mL |

Prepare onions, garlic and ginger by hand or one ingredient at a time in a food processor. Combine with sugar, sherry, soy sauce and Chinese Five Spice Powder in a non-metallic container. Roll tenderloins in the marinade. Cover and refrigerate one to three days. Turn the tenderloins every 12 hours.

Preheat the oven to 350°F (180°C). Place a large pan with 1 inch (2.5 cm) of water on oven's bottom rack. (This water ensures tender, juicy tenderloins.) For easy clean up, line a small roasting pan with foil and arrange meat and marinade on it. Roast, uncovered, 40-45 minutes. Remove from oven, cool, wrap and refrigerate until firm. Can be stored in the refrigerator for up to a week or frozen for future parties, picnics or cottage weekends. The meat slices well while still slightly frozen. Slice ¼ inch (0.5 cm) thick and arrange in overlapping rows on a platter around a bowl of chutney or hot mustard as an hors d'oeuvre.

**60 thin slices for an hors d'oeuvre**

**TIP:** To serve as a hot entrée, slice a little thicker and serve with rice, stir-fried water chestnuts and snow peas.

**Serves 8-10 as an entrée**

# Devilled Clams

*Devilishly delicious!*

| | | | |
|---|---|---|---|
| 2 | tablespoons onion, chopped | 30 | mL |
| 1½ | tablespoons butter | 25 | mL |
| 1½ | teaspoons flour | 7 | mL |
| ¼ | teaspoon salt | 1 | mL |
| | Dash of pepper | | |
| 1 | can (5 oz/142 g) clams or baby clams, minced | 1 | |
| | Milk | | |
| 2 | teaspoons parsley, minced | 10 | mL |
| 2 | hard-cooked eggs, chopped | 2 | |
| 1 | cup buttered bread crumbs | 250 | mL |
| | Paprika | | |

Preheat oven to 400°F (200°C). Sauté onions in butter until tender.
Add flour, salt and pepper; blend. Drain clams and add enough milk
to clam liquor to make 1 cup (250 mL). Add to flour mixture and
stir. Cook over medium heat until sauce thickens, stirring constantly. Add parsley, eggs and clams; mix well. Remove from heat.
Turn into large scallop shells or a shallow ovenproof dish. Sprinkle
buttered crumbs on top, dust with paprika and bake for 15 minutes
or until browned. Pass with crackers as an hors d'oeuvre.
**Makes 2 cups (500 mL)**

# Hot Broccoli Dip

*Serve in a hollowed-out bread round at your next party!*

| | | |
|---|---|---|
| 1 | bunch broccoli or 1 package (10 oz/283 g) frozen chopped broccoli | 1 |
| ¼ | cup butter, melted | 50 mL |
| 1 | onion, chopped | 1 |
| 6 | ounces Boursin or herb and garlic Rondelé cheese | 200 g |
| ¾ | pound fresh mushrooms, chopped | 375 g |
| 1 | can (10 oz/284 mL) condensed mushroom soup | 1 |

If using fresh broccoli, cook until crisp tender, drain and chop. If using frozen broccoli, cook briefly and drain. Sauté chopped mushrooms in 2 tablespoons (30 mL) of the butter until all the liquid is absorbed. Combine all ingredients over low heat and cook until cheese is melted. Serve hot or warm with French or pumpernickel bread, melba toast or crudités.

**VARIATION:** This mixture is an excellent filling for cocktail tartlettes or quiche.

**Makes about 3 cups (750 mL)**

# Dips for Crudités

*Really quick dips for raw vegetables.*

## Cheater Curry Dip

| | | |
|---|---|---|
| ½ | cup mayonnaise or salad dressing, regular or light | 125 mL |
| ½ | cup sour cream, regular or light | 125 mL |
| 2 | tablespoons curry powder | 30 mL |

Mix well and refrigerate until serving time. Amazingly good and takes 10 seconds!

## Sweet and Saucy Cheese Dip

| | | |
|---|---|---|
| 8 | ounces cream cheese, regular or light | 250 g |
| ¼-½ | cup peach and pepper relish (p. 192), or chutney or chili sauce | 50-125 mL |

Process in a food processor or blend together well.

## Pesto Mayo

| | | |
|---|---|---|
| 1 | cup mayonnaise, regular or light | 250 mL |
| 3 | tablespoons pesto (commercial or "Our Pesto"—p. 194) | 45 mL |

Mix well and refrigerate until serving time. Great on sandwiches, too!

## Roasted Red Pepper Dip

| | | |
|---|---|---|
| 1 | cup mayonnaise, regular or light | 250 mL |
| | or | |
| 8 | ounces cream cheese, regular or light | 250 g |
| 1-2 | large roasted red peppers (bottled or your own—p. 25) | 1-2 |

Process in a food processor until well blended. Great on sandwiches, too.

# Super Nachos

*A dig-in snack for a crowd!*

| | | | |
|---|---|---|---|
| 1 | pound ground beef (optional) | 500 | g |
| 1 | medium onion, chopped | 1 | |
| ½ | teaspoon salt | 2 | mL |
| 1 | can (14 oz/398 mL) refried beans | 1 | |
| 1 | can (4 oz/114 mL) green chillies, drained and chopped | 1 | |
| 1½ | cups Monterey Jack cheese, shredded | 375 | mL |
| 1 | cup Cheddar cheese, shredded | 250 | mL |
| ¾ | cup medium hot taco sauce | 175 | mL |
| 1 | cup sour cream, regular or light | 250 | mL |
| ¼ | cup green onion, chopped | 50 | mL |
| 1 | cup ripe olives, chopped | 250 | mL |
| 1 | large avocado | 1 | |
| 1 | tablespoon lemon or lime juice | 15 | mL |

Preheat oven to 400°F (200°C). In a frying pan, brown beef and onion. Drain and sprinkle lightly with salt. Spread refried beans evenly in a 9" × 13" (3.5 L) buttered baking dish. Layer with meat, green chillies, then cheeses. Drizzle taco sauce over all. Bake for about 20 minutes, until cheese is melted and beginning to bubble. Do not brown. Remove from oven; cover with dollops of sour cream. Use the whole cup. Cut avocado in small cubes and sprinkle with lemon or lime juice. Sprinkle the green onions, olives and avocado over all. Serve hot with oven-crisp tortilla chips.
**Serves 10-16**

# Old El Paso Tortilla Dip

*This makes a delicious dip to be served with your favourite corn, taco or tortilla chips.*

| 1 | can (14 oz/398 mL) refried beans, mashed | 1 | |
| 2-3 | ripe avocados, chopped | 2-3 | |
| 3 | tablespoons lemon juice | 45 | mL |
| ½ | teaspoon salt | 2 | mL |
| ¼ | teaspoon pepper | 1 | mL |
| 1 | cup sour cream, regular or light | 250 | mL |
| ½ | cup mayonnaise, regular or light | 125 | mL |
| 1 | package taco seasoning | 35 | g |
| 1 | can (4 oz/114 mL) green chillies, drained and chopped | 1 | |
| 1 | bunch green onions, chopped | 1 | |
| 2 | medium tomatoes, chopped | 2 | |
| 1 | cup pitted black olives, chopped | 250 | mL |
| 2 | cups Cheddar cheese, grated | 500 | mL |
| | plain corn chips, or tortilla chips | | |

Arrange beans in a large, flat serving bowl or platter to form first layer. Combine avocados, lemon juice, salt and pepper. Arrange over beans to form second layer. Combine sour cream, mayonnaise and taco seasoning to make third layer. Use green chillies for fourth layer. Mix green onions, tomatoes and black olives for fifth layer. Top with Cheddar cheese. Serve with several packages of chips.
**Serves about 20**

# Wonderful Ways with Cheese

## Golden Crown

*A delicious, quick and easy hors d'oeuvre—Ron's favourite.*

| | | |
|---|---|---|
| 8 | ounces Baby Gouda, Oka or Chaumes cheese, at room temperature | 250 g |
| 1 | package of Pillsbury crescent rolls | 235 g |
| | Dijon or sweet honey mustard | |

Preheat oven to 425°F (220°C). Peel wax from cheese if necessary. Unroll four crescent rolls and press together to form a rectangle. Spread dough with mustard. Place cheese in centre of dough, draw up corners and press together to form a fairly attractive package, making sure seams are sealed. Place on baking sheet and bake for 12-15 minutes or until pastry is puffy and golden. Serve on a garnished tray with small knives for cutting individual wedges.

**TIP:** Chili sauce, chutney, or peach and pepper relish (p. 192) may be substituted for mustard, and will produce a variety of taste treats.

## Camembert en Croûte

| | | |
|---|---|---|
| ¼ | package (14½ oz/411 g) puff pastry | ¼ |
| 1 | small round of Camembert or Brie (supermarket kind) | 1 |
| 1 | egg yolk, beaten with 1 tablespoon (15 mL) water | 1 |

Preheat oven to 425°F (220°C). Roll out pastry as thin as possible. Place cheese on pastry and, with a knife, cut out a round slightly larger than the cheese round. Wrap remaining pastry around the cheese, sealing around the circumference of the base. A small pastry cut-out may be reserved for a decoration on top. Brush pastry with egg wash. Bake on a small baking sheet for 10-15 minutes or until pastry is golden brown. Remove from oven and let sit 5 minutes until set. Serve with apple wedges.

# Chinese Cheese

| | | |
|---|---|---|
| 8 | ounces cream cheese, regular or light | 250 g |
| ½ | cup Teriyaki sauce | 125 mL |
| | or | |
| ½ | cup soy sauce sweetened with | 125 mL |
| | 4 tablespoons (60 mL) sugar | |
| ⅓ | cup sesame seeds, toasted | 75 mL |

Marinate cheese in Teriyaki sauce 1-3 days, turning it over from time to time. Place toasted seeds on a piece of foil. Remove cheese from marinade and roll in seeds. Place on serving dish and sprinkle with any remaining seeds. Serve with crackers.

# Buttered Brie

| | | |
|---|---|---|
| 1 | small round of Brie or Camembert (supermarket kind) | 1 |
| 2 | tablespoons butter, melted | 30 mL |
| ½ | cup almonds, slivered or sliced | 125 mL |

Preheat oven to 350°F (180°C). Bake cheese in oven on small greased baking sheet for 10-15 minutes until soft and warm. Meanwhile, sauté almonds in butter until golden brown. Place warm cheese on a small serving dish with a rim. Pour butter and almonds over cheese. Serve immediately with crackers and apple slices.

# Warm Brie

Heat individual wedges of Brie in oven or microwave until cheese begins to melt. Serve on garnished lettuce leaves as an appetizer or with prepared grapes, apple and pear wedges, and flat bread as dessert.

# Tart and Tangy

| 8 | ounces cream cheese, regular or light | 250 | g |
|---|---|---|---|
|   | or |   |   |
| 1 | wedge of Brie or Camembert or Cambozola | 1 |   |
|   | Generous dollops of Mrs. Smith's Famous Peach and Pepper Relish (p. 192) |   |   |

Toss "generous dollops" of peach and pepper relish over cheese and serve with crackers. It really is this simple!

# Potted Cheese

*This will keep in the refrigerator a lot longer than those old pieces!*

Gather together all the old wizened ends of cheese you've been collecting in the refrigerator. Trim if necessary. Grate or process in the food processor with steel blade until fine. Moisten with brandy, sherry or port. Add chili sauce, chutney, or peach and pepper relish (p. 192) to taste.

# Sandi's Cheese

*This is a sleeper—the taste is wonderful!*

| 1 | cup Hellman's mayonnaise | 250 | mL |
|---|---|---|---|
| 1 | cup old Cheddar cheese, grated | 250 | mL |
| 1 | onion, chopped | 1 |   |
| 1 | tablespoon butter | 15 | mL |

Preheat oven to 350°F (180°C). Sauté chopped onion in butter until translucent. Add remaining ingredients and mix well. Bake in a small baking dish for 20 minutes. Serve warm with your favourite crackers.

**TIP:** Try adding a can of crab or baby shrimp, well drained.

# Soups and Starters

# Potage St. Germaine

*A delicious soup from the old St. Germaine Hotel in St. Cloud, Minnesota. Serve hot or cold.*

| | | | |
|---|---|---|---|
| 2 | cans (each 10 oz/284 mL) chicken broth, undiluted | 2 | |
| 1 | small onion, grated | 1 | |
| 1 | large carrot, chopped | 1 | |
| 1 | large lettuce leaf, chopped | 1 | |
| 1 | tablespoon fresh mint or 1 teaspoon (5 mL) dried mint | 15 | mL |
| 1 | teaspoon sugar | 5 | mL |
| 2 | cups frozen peas | 500 | mL |
| | Salt and pepper to taste | | |
| | Dash of nutmeg | | |
| 1 | cup whipping cream or 2% evaporated milk | 250 | mL |

**GARNISHES:**
fresh dill, snipped
fresh chives, snipped
sour cream

In medium saucepan, combine broth, onion, carrot, lettuce, mint and sugar. Cook until vegetables are tender. Add frozen peas, salt, pepper and nutmeg. Cook 2 minutes. Purée in blender. Set aside and cool. When ready to use, add the whipping cream or evaporated milk. Serve chilled or, if you prefer, heat gently. Garnish with dill or chives and sour cream.
**Serves 8**

# Mushroom and Leek Bisque

*Divine! Make enough for seconds!*

| 3 | tablespoons butter | 45 | mL |
|---|---|---|---|
| 3 | large leeks, washed well and sliced, white part only | 3 | |
| ½ | pound firm white mushrooms, sliced | 250 | g |
| 2 | tablespoons flour | 30 | mL |
| 1 | teaspoon salt | 5 | mL |
| | Pinch of cayenne | | |
| | Freshly ground black pepper | | |
| | Pinch of basil or tarragon | | |
| 1 | cup chicken broth* | 250 | mL |
| 1 | cup milk | 250 | mL |
| 2 | cups 18% cream | 500 | mL |
| 1-2 | tablespoons sherry | 15-30 | mL |

In 1 tablespoon (15 mL) of the butter, sauté leeks until tender over low heat. Remove leeks and sauté sliced mushrooms in remaining butter until tender. Into mushrooms, blend flour, salt, cayenne and other spices. Gradually stir in chicken broth, milk and cream or evaporated milk. Cook, stirring until mixture just begins to come to a boil. Add leeks and sherry; adjust seasoning to taste. Simmer for 10 minutes before serving. Flavour improves if you can refrigerate for one day and then reheat. Just before pouring bisque into bowls, you may wish to stir in a tablespoon or two of butter—do not cook after this point.
**Serves 8**

**\*HOMEMADE CHICKEN BROTH:** Cover any assortment of chicken parts with water in a large pot. Add salt, sprigs of parsley, a couple of bay leaves, a couple of chopped carrots, a couple of onions, peeled and chopped in half, and some celery leaves. Bring to a boil, skim scum and simmer for several hours. Strain. Refrigerate so that you can remove most of the fat from the top before using.

**TIP:** For a lighter soup replace the milk and cream with 2% evaporated milk.

# Bay Scallops Chowder

*A meal in itself!*

| | | | |
|---|---|---|---|
| 3 | medium potatoes, diced | 3 | |
| 1 | small carrot, chopped | 1 | |
| 1 | large stalk celery, chopped | 1 | |
| 1 | medium onion, chopped | 1 | |
| 2 | cups chicken stock | 500 | mL |
| ½ | teaspoon salt | 2 | mL |
| ¼ | teaspoon pepper | 1 | mL |
| ½ | bay leaf | ½ | |
| ½ | teaspoon thyme | 2 | mL |
| 1 | pound scallops | 500 | g |
| ½ | pound mushrooms, sliced | 250 | g |
| 2 | tablespoons butter | 30 | mL |
| ½ | cup dry white wine | 125 | mL |
| 1 | cup whipping cream or | 250 | mL |
| | 2% evaporated milk | | |
| 2 | tablespoons parsley, chopped | 30 | mL |
| | Dash of paprika | | |

Place vegetables in large pot, cover with chicken stock and bring
to a boil. Add salt, pepper, bay leaf and thyme. Lower heat and
simmer, covered, until vegetables are very tender. Remove bay leaf
and transfer mixture to blender. Whirl until smooth. Meanwhile sauté
mushrooms in butter. Add scallops and wine; cook for 1 minute
only. Stir in cream or evaporated milk. Pour vegetable purée over
scallop mixture. Heat through and serve with parsley and paprika.
**Serves 4**

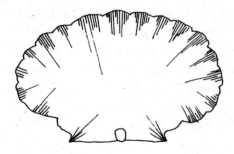

# Roasted Red Pepper Soup

*A refreshing soup with a subtle blend of flavours.*

| | | |
|---|---|---|
| 2 | tablespoons butter or olive oil | 30 mL |
| 2 | medium onions, diced | 2 |
| 3 | garlic cloves, minced | 3 |
| 4 | large sweet red peppers, roasted,* sliced and seeded or 1 jar (12 oz/313 mL) roasted red peppers | 4 |
| 3 | cups chicken stock or broth | 750 mL |
| 1 | bay leaf | 1 |
| 2 | tablespoons butter | 30 mL |
| 2 | tablespoons flour | 30 mL |
| ½ | cup whipping cream or 2% evaporated milk | 125 mL |
| 6 | tablespoons sour cream (optional) Chives, chopped | 90 mL |

Sauté onion and garlic in butter or oil for 2 minutes. Add peppers and sauté for 2 additional minutes without browning. Add chicken stock and bay leaf. Cover and simmer for 30 minutes. Remove bay leaf and check the seasonings. Mix the butter with the flour to form a beurre manié and add to soup a little bit at a time, stirring constantly. Cook about 5 minutes more or until thickened. Cool. Purée in blender or processor. Chill, add cream or evaporated milk. Garnish with a dollop of sour cream and a sprinkle of chives, if desired. **Serves 6**

**\*TO ROAST RED PEPPERS:** Preheat broiler on high. Cut peppers in quarters, lengthwise. Discard stems, seeds, and ribs. Place peppers, skin side up, on baking sheet about 2 inches (5 cm) from heat until skins are blackened and blistered—8-10 minutes. Remove to a bowl and cover or place in a brown paper bag. Skins should slip off easily when the peppers have cooled.

**VARIATION:** This soup can also be made with fresh, sweet red peppers.

# Cold Cream of Asparagus Soup

*A springtime treat!*

| | | | |
|---|---|---|---|
| 1 | pound asparagus | 500 | g |
| 2 | cans (each 10 oz/284 mL) chicken broth, undiluted | 2 | |
| 1 | tablespoon butter | 15 | mL |
| 1 | tablespoon flour | 15 | mL |
| | Juice of ½ lemon | | |
| | Pepper to taste | | |
| 1 | cup whipping cream or 2% evaporated milk | 250 | mL |

Cook uncut asparagus in chicken broth until limp. Remove and set aside. Prepare a roux with the butter and flour, adding a little broth. Add roux to remaining chicken broth and heat until slightly thickened. Reserve 4 asparagus spears and cut into pieces. Purée remaining asparagus in a food processor or blender until smooth. Return purée plus cut-up pieces to the thickened broth and mix well. Remove from heat, add the lemon juice, cream or evaporated milk and season to taste. Chill for at least 6 hours.

**Serves 6**

# Mushroom and Scallion Soup

*Fantastic!*

| | | | |
|---|---|---|---|
| ¼ | cup butter | 50 | mL |
| 5 | bunches scallions or green onions— yes, 5 entire bunches—chopped | 5 | |
| 1 | teaspoon white pepper | 5 | mL |
| 5 | cups chicken stock | 1.25 | L |
| 1 | pound mushrooms, thinly sliced | 500 | g |
| 1¼ | cups 18% cream or 2% evaporated milk | 300 | mL |
| 4 | tablespoons whipping cream, whipped (optional) Dash of cayenne pepper | 60 | mL |

Melt butter in a large saucepan. Add onions and pepper. Sauté for 10 minutes. Add stock and bring to a boil. Cover and simmer for 10 minutes. Add half of the mushrooms and soak for one minute. Purée in blender or food processor until smooth. The soup may be frozen at this point. Add cream or evaporated milk and heat. Drop in remaining mushrooms and cook slowly until tender. Serve with a dollop of whipped cream (if desired) and a sprinkle of cayenne pepper. **Serves 8-10**

# Carrot Soup

*A hearty soup—good for a ski lunch.*

| | | |
|---|---|---|
| ¼ | cup butter or oil | 50 mL |
| ½ | cup onion, chopped | 125 mL |
| 2 | cups carrots, thinly sliced | 500 mL |
| ¼ | cup long-grain rice, uncooked | 50 mL |
| 3 | cups chicken stock or 3 chicken bouillon cubes dissolved in 2 cups boiling water | 750 mL |
| ½ | teaspoon salt | 2 mL |
| 1 | teaspoon curry powder | 5 mL |
| 2 | cups milk | 500 mL |

In a medium saucepan, sauté onions in butter or oil until translucent. Add carrots and rice; toss until well coated. Add curry and chicken stock. Simmer until carrots are tender and rice is cooked. Add salt. Purée, fine or coarse, ⅓ at a time in the blender or food processor. Return to pan, add milk and heat gently. Do not boil.

**Serves 6**

# Cream of Asparagus Soup

*Freeze the purée and try this soup in the winter.*

| | | | |
|---|---|---|---|
| 1 | large onion, chopped fine | 1 | |
| 2 | tablespoons butter | 30 | mL |
| 3 | tablespoons flour | 45 | mL |
| 4 | cups chicken broth | 1 | L |
| 1 | cup milk | 250 | mL |
| 1½ | pounds asparagus, trimmed | 750 | g |
| | Salt and pepper | | |
| 1 | cup whipping cream or | | |
| | 2% evaporated milk | 250 | mL |
| | Gruyère cheese, grated | | |

Trim tips from asparagus and reserve for garnish. Cut stalks into 1-inch (2.5-cm) pieces. Melt butter in a saucepan and cook onion until limp. Add flour and cook roux over low heat, without browning, for 4 minutes. Add stock and milk and bring to a boil. Add asparagus stalks, cover, reduce heat and simmer 30 minutes.

Blanch asparagus tips. Drain and refresh under cold water. Set aside. Purée stock, milk, asparagus stalks and onion in food processor. Put through sieve for a smoother soup. Soup can be frozen at this point. Return purée to saucepan and stir in cream or evaporated milk. Season. Do not allow the soup to boil. Garnish each serving with asparagus tips and a sprinkling of Gruyère cheese.
**Serves 6**

# Cream of Leek Soup with Stilton Cheese

*The flavour leaps out of the bowl!*

| | | | |
|---|---|---|---|
| 2 | tablespoons butter | 30 | mL |
| 1 | shallot, finely chopped | 1 | |
| 2 | leeks, chopped | 2 | |
| 1 | potato, diced | 1 | |
| 2 | cups chicken stock | 500 | mL |
| 1½ | cups 35% cream or 10% cream or 2% evaporated milk | 375 | mL |
| | Salt and pepper to taste | | |
| ⅛ | teaspoon nutmeg | 0.5 | mL |
| 1 | teaspoon lemon juice or to taste | 5 | mL |
| 2 | ounces Stilton cheese, crumbled | 60 | g |

Melt butter in a deep pot. Add shallot and leeks and sweat them until translucent. Add potatoes and chicken stock. Simmer briskly until stock is reduced by half and potatoes are cooked. Purée in blender. In a separate saucepan, simmer and reduce cream or evaporated milk until it begins to thicken. Add to soup and bring to boil. Remove from heat and season with salt, pepper, nutmeg and lemon juice. Pour into warm soup bowls and top each serving with crumbled Stilton.

**Serves 6**

# Swamp Soup

*This is a favourite soup served at Rachel McLeod's Herb Farm, Puslinch, Ontario.*

| | | | |
|---|---|---|---|
| 1 | cup fresh or canned tomatoes, chopped | 250 | mL |
| 3 | tablespoons onion, chopped | 45 | mL |
| 3 | tablespoons butter | 45 | mL |
| ½ | cup fresh mushrooms, chopped | 125 | mL |
| 1 | tablespoon flour | 15 | mL |
| ½ | tablespoon honey | 7 | mL |
| 1 | garlic clove, minced | 1 | |
| 4 | cups beef and vegetable stock or beef bouillon | 1 | L |
| 1 | teaspoon fresh basil (or ½ teaspoon/ 2 mL dried) | 5 | mL |
| 1 | teaspoon fresh thyme (or ½ teaspoon/ 2 mL dried) | 5 | mL |
| ½ | teaspoon fresh rosemary (or ¼ teaspoon/ 1 mL dried) | 2 | mL |
| | salt and pepper to taste | | |
| 2 | tablespoons cream cheese, grated (optional) | 30 | mL |
| | Fresh parsley | | |
| | Fresh mint | | |

Sauté onions and mushrooms in butter until limp. Sprinkle flour on top. Add garlic and honey. Stir in stock and herbs. Bring to a boil and taste for seasonings. Add tomato and simmer for 30 minutes. Just before serving, grate cream cheese* into soup. Garnish with chopped parsley and chopped fresh mint.
**Serves 6**

**\*TIP:** Instead of grating cream cheese put through a garlic press.

# Zucchini Soup

*Heart-warming on a cold day!*

| | | |
|---|---|---|
| ½ | pound bacon, diced and browned | 250 g |
| 1 | medium onion, chopped | 1 |
| 1 | green pepper, diced | 1 |
| 3 | cups celery chunks | 750 mL |
| 2 | cans (each 10 oz/284 mL) sliced mushrooms | 2 |
| 1 | quart fresh tomatoes or 1 can (28 oz/796 mL) | 1 L |
| 1 | can (14 oz/398 mL) tomato sauce | 1 |
| 5-6 | zucchini, sliced | 5-6 |
| 1 | cup water | 250 mL |
| ½ | teaspoon salt | 2 mL |
| ¼ | teaspoon pepper | 1 mL |
| 1 | teaspoon basil | 5 mL |
| 1 | teaspoon sugar | 5 mL |

Sauté onion, green pepper and celery in 2 tablespoons (30 mL) of bacon fat until onion is transparent. Add remaining ingredients and simmer until zucchini is crisp tender. Adjust seasonings. Try some Parmesan cheese sprinkled on top.

**Serves 6**

# Lentil and Barley Soup

*A meal in itself with crusty, brown bread and a salad.*

| | | | |
|---|---|---|---|
| 1 | pound ground beef | 500 | g |
| 1 | cup split yellow or green lentils | 250 | mL |
| ¼ | cup pearl barley | 50 | mL |
| 6 | cups stock or bouillon | 1.5 | L |
| 1 | large onion, chopped | 1 | |
| 1 | large carrot, diced | 1 | |
| 1 | large celery rib, diced | 1 | |
| 1 | garlic clove, minced | 1 | |
| 2 | cups tomatoes, canned or fresh | 500 | mL |
| 1 | bay leaf | 1 | |
| | Large pinch of thyme | | |
| | Basil to taste | | |
| | Salt and pepper to taste | | |
| | Fresh parsley, chopped | | |

Brown beef slightly in a dutch oven or other large heavy pan. Pour off fat. Add lentils, barley and stock. Simmer for ½ hour. Add remaining ingredients and simmer for about 1½ hours. Add salt and pepper to taste.

**Serves 6-8**

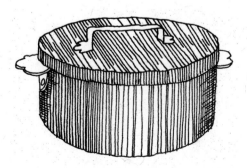

# Borscht

*This colourful beet soup is delicious served hot or cold. A dollop of sour cream and a lavish sprinkling of freshly chopped parsley are perfect compliments in individual serving dishes.*

| | | |
|---|---|---|
| ½ | cup carrots | 125 mL |
| 1 | cup onions | 250 mL |
| 2 | cups beets | 500 mL |
| | Boiling water | |
| 1 | tablespoon butter | 15 mL |
| 2 | cups rich beef stock | 500 mL |
| 1 | cup cabbage, finely shredded | 250 mL |
| 1 | tablespoon vinegar | 15 mL |
| | Salt and pepper | |
| 6 | tablespoons sour cream | 90 mL |
| 3 | tablespoons fresh parsley, finely chopped | 45 mL |

Wash and peel carrots, onions and beets. Chop until very fine. Place in a large pot and pour enough boiling water to just cover vegetables. Simmer gently, with cover, for about 20 minutes. Add butter, beef stock, cabbage and vinegar. Simmer for 15 minutes more. Season to taste. Pour into individual serving bowls and garnish with a dollop of sour cream and parsley.

**Serves 6**

# Corn Chowder

*A hearty soup!*

| | | | |
|---|---|---|---|
| 1½ | cups potatoes, peeled and diced | 375 | mL |
| ½ | cup water | 125 | mL |
| 6 | slices bacon, fried and chopped | 6 | |
| ½ | cup onion, chopped | 125 | mL |
| ¼ | cup green pepper, chopped | 50 | mL |
| 1 | tablespoon butter | 15 | mL |
| 2 | cups creamed corn | 500 | mL |
| 1 | can (12 oz/350 mL) corn niblets | 1 | |
| 1 | can (10 oz/284 mL) mushroom soup (optional) | 1 | |
| | Salt and pepper to taste | | |
| ½ | teaspoon curry powder | 2 | mL |
| 4 | cups whole milk or 10% cream | 1 | L |

Cook potatoes in ½ cup (125 mL) water until tender. Drain. Sauté onion and green pepper in butter until soft. In large pot, combine all ingredients except the bacon. Heat thoroughly. Serve with bacon on top.
**Serves 8**

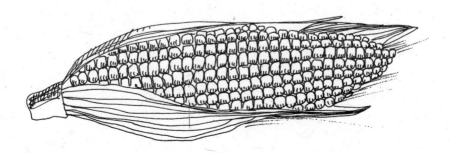

# Curried Broccoli Soup

*A perfect start to a dinner party.*

| | | | |
|---|---|---|---|
| 1 | tablespoon butter | 15 | mL |
| ½ | cup celery, chopped | 125 | mL |
| ¼ | cup onions, chopped | 50 | mL |
| 1 | bunch broccoli, chopped | 1 | |
| 1 | cup chicken broth | 250 | mL |
| 1 | cup milk | 250 | mL |
| 1 | cup 18% cream | 250 | mL |
| ¼ | teaspoon white pepper | 1 | mL |
| ¼ | teaspoon curry powder—or to taste | 1 | mL |
| | Salt to taste | | |

Cook celery and onions slowly in butter for about 5 minutes. Do not brown. Add broccoli and broth and simmer until tender. Purée in blender or food processor. Return to pan and add remaining ingredients. Heat gently and serve. Can be made in advance and reheated carefully.

**Serves 6**

**TIP:** For a lighter soup replace the milk and cream with 2% evaporated milk.

# Shrimp and Artichoke Vinaigrette

| 2 | cans (each 15 oz/426 mL) artichoke hearts, drained and halved | 2 | |
|---|---|---|---|
| 1½ | pounds medium shrimp, cooked and peeled | 750 | g |
| ¼ | cup vegetable oil | 50 | mL |
| ¼ | cup olive oil | 50 | mL |
| ¼ | cup wine vinegar | 50 | mL |
| 2 | tablespoons Dijon mustard | 30 | mL |
| 2 | tablespoons chives, chopped | 30 | mL |
| 2 | tablespoons scallions or onions, minced | 30 | mL |
| ½ | teaspoon salt | 2 | mL |
| ½ | teaspoon sugar | 2 | mL |
| | Dash of pepper | | |
| 6 | lettuce cups | 6 | |

Chill artichokes and shrimp thoroughly. Combine remaining ingredients. Marinate artichokes and shrimp in dressing for about 6 hours in refrigerator. Drain. Place lettuce cups on individual plates. Top with shrimp and artichoke mixture and serve as a starter.
**Serves 6**

**VARIATION:** Pass with toothpicks as an hors d'oeuvre.

# Coquilles St. Jacques Cardinal

| | | | |
|---|---|---|---|
| 1 | pound scallops | 500 | g |
| ½ | cup white wine | 125 | mL |
| 1 | small bouquet garni | 1 | |
| 1 | onion, sliced | 1 | |
| | Salt and pepper to taste | | |
| 1 | pound cooked shrimp | 500 | g |
| ½ | pound mushrooms, sliced | 250 | g |
| 3 | tablespoons butter | 45 | mL |

**SAUCE**

| | | | |
|---|---|---|---|
| 3 | tablespoons butter | 45 | mL |
| 3 | tablespoons flour | 45 | mL |
| 1½ | cups 10% cream | 375 | mL |
| ½ | cup poaching liquid | 125 | mL |
| 2 | egg yolks | 2 | |

**DUCHESSE POTATOES**

| | | | |
|---|---|---|---|
| 3 | cups hot mashed potatoes | 750 | mL |
| 2 | egg yolks | 2 | |
| ¼ | cup 10% cream | 50 | mL |
| 2 | tablespoons butter | 30 | mL |
| | Salt and pepper to taste | | |
| | Pinch of nutmeg | | |
| | Thin slices of tomatoes and grated Parmesan for garnish | | |

Preheat oven to 375°F (190°C). In saucepan, pour white wine over scallops. Add bouquet garni, onion, salt, pepper and enough water to cover. Cook for 6-8 minutes. Remove scallops and slice thinly. Reduce poaching liquid to ½ cup (125 mL) and strain. Meanwhile, sauté mushrooms in melted butter. Combine scallops, shrimp and mushrooms. To prepare sauce, melt butter in saucepan, add flour and mix. Slowly add cream and poaching liquid. Add some of this hot mixture to egg yolks, then carefully stir egg yolk mixture back into sauce. Cook slowly for 2 minutes; remove from heat. Add 2 cups (500 mL) of this sauce to scallops, mushrooms and shrimp. Fill scallop shells with this mixture. Make Duchesse potatoes by adding egg yolks, cream, butter and seasoning to mashed potatoes. Mix well. Pipe potatoes around edge of shells. Top with thin slice of tomato and sprinkle with Parmesan cheese. Heat and brown lightly for 15-20 minutes.
**Serves 6**

# Lime-Marinated Scallops in Coconut Sauce

*An incredibly good first course!*

| | | | |
|---|---|---|---|
| ½ | cup fresh lime juice | 125 | mL |
| 4 | dashes Tabasco sauce | 4 | |
| 1 | teaspoon salt | 5 | mL |
| 1 | teaspoon white pepper, freshly ground | 5 | mL |
| 1 | pound Bay or Sea scallops, fresh or frozen, thoroughly defrosted, drained and cut into 1-inch (2.5-cm) cubes | 500 | g |
| ¼ | cup hot water | 50 | mL |
| 3½ | ounces coconut cream, available at West Indian shops | 98 | g |
| ½ | cup sour cream | 125 | mL |
| 1 | tablespoon 18% cream | 15 | mL |
| 6 | teaspoons scallions, finely chopped, green and white | 30 | mL |

Mix lime juice, Tabasco, salt and pepper in a deep glass or ceramic bowl. Add scallops and toss to coat well. Cover bowl and marinate in refrigerator for at least 2 hours, stirring occasionally, until they are white and opaque, indicating that they are fully "cooked". When ready to serve, combine water and coconut cream in a blender or processor for 30 seconds until well mixed. Remove to mixing bowl. Add sour cream and table cream. Blend well. Drain scallops and add to sauce. Thin with a little marinade if necessary. Serve on scallop shells or a bed of lettuce garnished with the scallions and parsley or watercress.

**Serves 6 to 8**

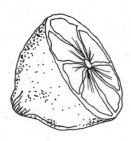

# Lemony Veal Terrine

*Fantastic hot-weather food with a fresh, light, lemony taste.*

| | | |
|---|---|---|
| 2 | pounds lean veal shoulder or shank, cubed | 1 kg |
| 2 | quarts water | 2 L |
| 2 | tablespoons chicken bouillon powder | 30 mL |
| 2-3 | lemons | 2-3 |
| 1 | large onion, sliced | 1 |
| 1 | small onion, grated | 1 |
| 1 | bunch parsley, finely minced | 1 |
| 3-4 | hard-cooked eggs, well chilled and sliced | 3-4 |
| | Salt and pepper to taste | |

Place veal, water, bouillon powder, juice and rind of one lemon, large onion and half of parsley in a large pot. Bring to a boil and simmer, uncovered, until liquid is reduced to 1 cup (250 mL). This will take about 4-6 hours. Cool. Grind or chop in food processor, being careful not to purée it. Add any remaining cooking liquid, remaining parsley, grated onion, ⅓-½ cup (75-125 mL) lemon juice, salt and pepper. Mix well. Butter a 9" × 5" (2 L) Pyrex loaf pan. Line bottom and sides with choice slices of egg. Pack veal mixture carefully into pan. Cover and chill at least 6 hours—overnight is better. Serve with mayonnaise, cucumber slices, tomatoes and watercress.
**Serves 8 or more**

**TIP:** Can be made days ahead or frozen. If freezing omit egg slices.

# Spinach and Seafood Terrine Supreme

*Served with a lemony, dill sauce.*

| | | | |
|---|---|---|---|
| 1 | pound raw scallops, fresh or frozen | 500 | g |
| ½ | pound raw shrimps, fresh or frozen | 250 | g |
| 2 | egg whites, cold | 2 | |
| 1 | teaspoon salt | 5 | mL |
| ¼ | teaspoon pepper | 1 | mL |
| | Dash of cayenne pepper | | |
| 1½ | cups whipping cream or 18% cream | 375 | mL |
| 1 | package (10 oz/283 mL) spinach, frozen | 1 | |
| ¼ | cup fresh dill, chopped | 50 | mL |

Preheat oven to 350°F (180°C). Pat scallops and shrimps dry with paper towels. Place in blender or food processor and blend until smooth. Blend in egg whites and seasonings. With machine running, add cream in a stream. Do not overmix. Remove all but ½ cup (125 mL) seafood from container. Wring out the spinach until dry and chop. Add spinach and dill to remaining seafood mixture in blender. Purée. Add seasonings if necessary. Spoon ½ plain seafood mixture into an 8" × 4" (1.5 L) buttered loaf pan. Add seafood/spinach purée, then spread remaining plain seafood mixture on top. Cover with buttered wax-paper. Place in a pan of boiling water and bake for 30-35 minutes, or until mixture is firm. Cool, remove from pan and chill.

## SAUCE

| | | | |
|---|---|---|---|
| 1 | cup mayonnaise, regular or light | 250 | mL |
| ¼ | cup lemon juice | 50 | mL |
| 1 | teaspoon Dijon mustard | 5 | mL |
| ¼ | cup fresh dill, chopped | 50 | mL |
| 2 | green onions, chopped | 2 | |

Combine all ingredients in blender or food processor. To serve, place a spoonful of sauce on a plate and cover with a slice of terrine. Garnish with dill and lemon. Serve as an appetizer or on black bread for sandwiches.

**Serves 6-10**

# Terrine of Sole and Salmon with Sherry Wine Vinegar Sauce

*Spectacular!*

| 12 | ounces spinach leaves | 375 g |
| 4-5 | sole fillets | 500 g |
| 1 | pound salmon, boned and skinned | 500 g |
| ½ | tablespoon lemon juice | 7 mL |
| 1 | scallion or shallot, finely chopped | 1 |
| 2 | egg whites | 2 |
| 6 | tablespoons whipping cream | 90 mL |
| | Dash of Tabasco | |
| | Salt and freshly ground pepper to taste | |
| | Parchment paper to line pan | |
| | Lemon, parsley or watercress for garnish | |

Preheat oven to 375°F (190°C). Cut parchment paper to fit bottom of 3-4 cup (750 mL-1 L) loaf pan. Butter the pan and line with the paper. Butter the paper also. Set aside 2-3 large spinach leaves to use in the sherry wine sauce. Blanch, rinse and squeeze dry the remainder of the spinach. Chop finely or coarsely purée. Wash fillets in lemon juice and cold water; dry. Line prepared pan with the sole crosswise and dark side up. Allow each piece of sole to hang over the side of pan. Reserve one fillet for the middle of the terrine. Purée salmon, a little at a time, in blender or processor. Add the egg whites and process again. Add cream, Tabasco, salt and pepper. Season well. Mix in scallion or shallot. Spoon ½ of the salmon mixture into the pan. Layer ½ of the spinach mixture over the salmon. Place the remaining sole fillet length-wise down the pan. Again spoon the remaining spinach over the fillet and finish with the rest of the salmon. Bang the terrine on the counter to settle the contents and cover with overhanging pieces of sole. Cover with well-buttered parchment paper. Can be assembled hours before baking. Bake in pan of hot water in oven for 45 minutes or until skewer comes out clean. Carefully drain off liquid. Let rest in pan until cool, then refrigerate until ready to serve. Turn out onto serving platter; garnish with lemon twists and fresh parsley or watercress. Serve with Sherry Wine Vinegar Mayonnaise (p. 43).

## SHERRY WINE VINEGAR MAYONNAISE

| 1½ | cups regular or light mayonnaise | 375 | mL |
| 1 | tablespoon Dijon mustard | 15 | mL |
| ¼ | cup sherry wine vinegar | 50 | mL |
| 2-3 | spinach leaves (saved from terrine) | 2-3 | |
| | Salt and freshly ground pepper to taste | | |

Combine mayonnaise, mustard, vinegar and spinach leaves in work bowl of food processor which has been fitted with metal blade. Process. Season with salt and pepper. To serve, ladle some sauce onto a serving plate and place a slice of terrine on top.
**Serves 12 as an appetizer, 8 as a lunch**

# Smoked Salmon in Horseradish Cream

*A spectacular first course or light lunch.*

| 8 | thin slices smoked salmon | 8 | |
| 1 | cup whipping cream, whipped | 250 | mL |
| 2 | tablespoons horseradish | 30 | mL |
| 1 | cup small cooked shrimps | 250 | mL |
| | Salt and pepper to taste | | |
| | Boston lettuce | | |
| 8 | lemon wedges | 8 | |
| | Fresh parsley | | |

Place leaves of lettuce on individual serving plates. Place one slice of salmon on each. Whip cream, stir in horseradish, shrimp, salt and pepper. Place a large spoonful of cream mixture on each slice of salmon. Garnish with lemon wedges and parsley.
**Serves 8**

# Gravlaks

*This delicious Norwegian delicacy is very simple to prepare. Frozen supermarket salmon is perfectly suitable.*

| | | | |
|---|---|---|---|
| 3-3½ | pounds salmon | 1.5 | kg |
| 1 | bunch fresh dill | 1 | |
| ¼ | cup coarse salt (pickling salt) | 50 | mL |
| ¼ | cup sugar | 50 | mL |
| 2 | tablespoons peppercorns, crushed | 30 | mL |

**SUGGESTED ACCOMPANIMENTS:** cream cheese, honey mustard, horseradish, rye bread

**SUGGESTED GARNISHES:** hard-boiled eggs, capers, lemons, limes, thinly sliced onion

Cut fish in half lengthwise and remove the backbone and small bones. Place half the fish, skin side down, in a large glass or enamel dish. Cover with dill and mixture of salt, sugar and pepper. Top with the other half of the fish, skin side up. Cover with foil. Set a heavy platter on it and weight with a heavy object. Refrigerate for 48 hours or up to 3 days. Turn fish a couple of times and baste with liquid which accumulates. When the gravlaks is finished, remove the fish from its marinade, scrape away the seasoning and pat dry with paper towels. Place the halves, skin side down, on a carving board and slice thinly on the diagonal, detaching each slice from the skin. Use as part of a "smorgasbord" or as an appetizer.
**Serves 16-20**

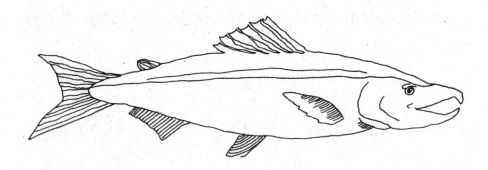

# Smoked Salmon Vinaigrette

*A good way to stretch smoked salmon and use salmon pieces.*

| | | |
|---|---|---|
| ½ | pound smoked salmon | 250 g |
| 2 | medium-sized potatoes, cooked and diced | 2 |
| 1 | tablespoon capers | 15 mL |
| 1 | tablespoon onion, minced | 15 mL |
| 2 | green onions, chopped | 2 |
| ¼ | cup stuffed green olives, sliced | 50 mL |
| ½ | cup herb and oil dressing | 125 mL |
| | Dill for garnish | |

Cut salmon into pieces; place in shallow dish. Layer the other
ingredients, except for dressing. Pour this on top, but do not stir.
Sprinkle with fresh dill and refrigerate for 1-2 hours. Bits and pieces
of smoked salmon may be purchased at the market and are quite
suitable for this dish. Serve as a first course, at a picnic or at a buffet
on pumpernickel bread.

**Serves 8**

# Bacon-Stuffed Avocados

*A sinful starter!*

| | | |
|---|---|---|
| 4 | avocados, ripe and unpeeled | 4 |
| | Lemon juice | |
| 4-6 | slices crisp bacon, crumbled | 4-6 |
| ¼ | cup butter | 50 mL |
| 2 | tablespoons brown sugar | 30 mL |
| 2 | tablespoons ketchup | 30 mL |
| 2 | tablespoons wine vinegar | 30 mL |
| 1 | teaspoon soy sauce | 5 mL |

Cut avocados in half. Remove pits and brush with lemon juice. Fill with bacon. Combine remaining ingredients and heat to boiling. Drizzle some sauce over avocados. You probably could get away with serving ¼ avocado per person, but it would only be half as sinful!
**Serves 8**

# Salads and Dressings

# Colourful Summer Salad

*Good with croissants and iced tea.*

| | | | |
|---|---|---|---|
| 1 | quart strawberries, washed, hulled and sliced | 1 | L |
| 4 | cups romaine lettuce, washed, dried and torn | 1 | L |

## DRESSING

| | | | |
|---|---|---|---|
| ½ | cup mayonnaise, regular or light | 125 | mL |
| ½ | cup sour cream, regular or light | 125 | mL |
| 1 | tablespoon poppy seeds | 15 | mL |
| 1 | tablespoon sesame seeds | 15 | mL |
| 1 | tablespoon sugar | 15 | mL |
| 1 | teaspoon lemon juice | 5 | mL |
| | Pinch of ginger | | |

Set out 8 salad plates and put ½ cup (125 mL) lettuce on each plate. Divide the strawberries evenly and place on top of lettuce. Drizzle with dressing and serve at once.

**Serves 8**

# Orange Pico Salad

*Colourful! Serve with pride.*

| | | |
|---|---|---|
| 5 | oranges, peeled, sliced and seeded | 5 |
| 1 | English cucumber, thinly sliced, unpeeled | 1 |
| 6 | cups spinach leaves, torn | 1.5 L |
| 2 | heads Bibb lettuce, torn | 2 |
| ½ | cup toasted walnuts, coarsely chopped | 125 mL |

## DRESSING

| | | |
|---|---|---|
| ½ | cup vegetable oil | 125 mL |
| ¼ | cup orange juice | 50 mL |
| 2 | tablespoons cider vinegar | 30 mL |
| 1½ | teaspoons sugar | 7 mL |
| ¼ | teaspoon salt | 1 mL |
| | Dash of pepper, freshly ground | |

Mix all the dressing ingredients together and refrigerate. Combine the lettuce and spinach in a large glass bowl and toss with dressing at serving time. Place ½ the oranges around the inside edges of the bowl. The next ring should be ½ the cucumber. Repeat. Sprinkle walnuts on top and serve.

**Serves 12**

# Oriental Chicken Salad

*To serve as a luncheon salad, crumble bacon on top and garnish with watercress and preserved kumquats.*

| | | |
|---|---|---|
| 2 | whole chicken breasts, cooked and cut into pieces | 2 |
| ⅓ | cup white wine | 75 mL |
| ¼ | cup soy sauce | 50 mL |
| 2 | teaspoons freshly grated ginger | 10 mL |
| 4-5 | cups mixed salad greens | 1-1.25 L |
| 6 | green onions, chopped | 6 |
| 1 | cup broccoli florets, cooked crisp | 250 mL |
| ½ | cup almonds, slivered or sliced | 125 mL |
| ¼ | cup sesame seeds, toasted | 50 mL |

**DRESSING**

| | | |
|---|---|---|
| ½ | cup salad oil | 125 mL |
| ¼ | cup white wine vinegar | 50 mL |
| 1 | tablespoon soy sauce | 15 mL |
| 2 | teaspoons dry mustard | 10 mL |
| 2 | teaspoons sugar | 10 mL |
| 2 | teaspoons freshly grated ginger | 10 mL |
| 1 | garlic clove, minced | 1 |
| | Dash of Tabasco | |

Prepare a marinade by mixing wine, soy sauce and ginger. Marinate chicken for at least 2 hours. Drain well. Put salad greens, onions, broccoli, almonds and chicken in a large salad bowl. Combine all dressing ingredients in a jar and shake well. Toss salad with dressing and sprinkle sesame seeds on top.

**Serves 6**

# Avocado and Orange Salad

## DRESSING

| | | | |
|---|---|---|---|
| ½ | cup salad oil | 125 | mL |
| ⅓ | cup orange juice | 75 | mL |
| 1 | tablespoon white wine vinegar | 15 | mL |
| 1 | small garlic clove, minced | 1 | |
| 1½ | tablespoons orange peel, grated | 25 | mL |
| 1½ | teaspoons basil | 7 | mL |
| 1 | teaspoon sugar | 5 | mL |
| ¼ | teaspoon salt | 1 | mL |
| | Pepper to taste | | |

## SALAD

| | | |
|---|---|---|
| 1½ | large heads romaine lettuce, torn | 1½ |
| 1 | can (10 oz/284 mL) mandarin oranges, drained | 1 |
| 2 | avocados, sliced | 2 |

Combine dressing ingredients at least one hour before serving. Pour over the salad and toss lightly.

**Serves 8-10**

# Layered Spinach Salad

*A lighter version of an old favourite. The salad stays crisp and fresh even though it's made a day in advance.*

| | | | |
|---|---|---|---|
| 1 | package (10 oz/284 g) fresh spinach, washed and dried | 1 | |
| | Salt and freshly ground pepper to taste | | |
| 3 | hard-cooked eggs, chopped | 3 | |
| 4 | ounces cooked ham, cut into strips | 125 | g |
| 1 | small iceberg lettuce, cut into strips | 1 | |
| 1 | package (12 oz/340 g) frozen peas | 1 | |
| 1 | red onion, thinly sliced and separated | 1 | |
| 1 | cup mayonnaise, regular or light | 250 | mL |
| ½ | cup sour cream, regular or light | 125 | mL |
| 1 | cup extra old Cheddar or Gruyère cheese, grated | 250 | mL |
| 4 | slices bacon, cooked and crumbled | 4 | |

Tear spinach into bite-sized pieces and place in a large, deep, glass salad bowl. Sprinkle with salt and pepper to taste. Layer on eggs, then ham, then iceberg lettuce. Sprinkle lightly with salt and pepper. Blanch peas for 2 minutes in boiling water, cool under cold water and drain thoroughly. Sprinkle on top of lettuce; arrange onion rings over peas. Combine mayonnaise with sour cream and spread over salad. Sprinkle with cheese. Cover and refrigerate overnight. Sprinkle with bacon just before serving; do not toss!
**Serves 12-14**

This salad is a meal in itself when served with fresh rolls or crisp French bread.

# Marinated Tomato Salad

*Easy but elegant. Use tomatoes at their best!*

| | | |
|---|---|---|
| 3 | large tomatoes, sliced | 3 |
| 1 | Spanish onion, thinly sliced and separated | 1 |
| ¼ | pound Feta cheese | 125 g |
| | Fresh basil, chives or green onions, chopped | |
| | Salt and pepper to taste | |

## DRESSING

| | | |
|---|---|---|
| ½ | cup oil | 125 mL |
| 2 | tablespoons vinegar or lemon juice | 30 mL |
| ½ | teaspoon salt | 2 mL |
| ½ | teaspoon pepper, freshly ground | 2 mL |
| 1 | small garlic clove, minced | 1 |
| 1 | teaspoon Dijon mustard | 5 mL |

Arrange one layer of tomatoes and one layer of onions in a fluted quiche dish or a large dish with sides. Crumble cheese over the layers. Sprinkle with chopped basil, chives or green onions, salt and pepper. Combine all ingredients for dressing in a covered jar and shake. Drizzle some over salad. Repeat until all ingredients are used up. Garnish with chopped chives or green onions and basil, cover and refrigerate.

**Serves 8-10**

# My Mom's Special Potato Salad

*Mother* does *know best!*

| | | | |
|---|---|---|---|
| 8 | large potatoes, cooked in jackets and cooled | 8 | |
| 2 | tablespoons butter | 30 | mL |
| 1 | tablespoon cornstarch | 15 | mL |
| ½ | cup milk | 125 | mL |
| ⅓ | cup sugar | 75 | mL |
| 1 | egg, beaten | 1 | |
| ¾ | teaspoon salt | 4 | mL |
| 1 | tablespoon celery seed | 15 | mL |
| ¼ | cup vinegar | 50 | mL |
| ¼ | teaspoon dry mustard | 1 | mL |
| ¼ | cup onion, chopped | 50 | mL |
| ½ | cup mayonnaise, regular or light | 125 | mL |
| 3 | hard-boiled eggs | 3 | |

Peel and chop potatoes into bite-sized pieces. In a saucepan, melt butter and add cornstarch to make a paste. Add milk, sugar and egg and heat until mixture is thick. Add salt, celery seed, dry mustard and, lastly, the vinegar. Heat until mixture begins to bubble; remove from the stove. Let cool one half-hour in the refrigerator. Add the chopped onion and the mayonnaise. Add dressing to the potatoes and toss well. Chop hard-boiled eggs and add to the salad. Add chopped celery if desired.

**Serves 12**

# Tabbouleh

*Be adventurous—try it!*

Bulgar wheat is readily available in health food stores.

| | | | |
|---|---|---|---|
| 1 | cup bulgar wheat (cracked wheat) | 250 | mL |
| 1 | cup cold water | 250 | mL |
| ½ | cup parsley, chopped | 125 | mL |
| ¼ | cup green onions, sliced | 50 | mL |
| 1-2 | garlic cloves, minced | 1-2 | |
| ½ | cup fresh mint, chopped | 125 | mL |
| 2-3 | tomatoes | 2-3 | |
| ¼ | cup oil | 50 | mL |
| ¼ | cup lemon juice | 50 | mL |
| | Salt and pepper to taste | | |
| 6-8 | leaves of romaine or Boston lettuce | 6-8 | |

Rinse wheat in lots of cold water and drain. Combine with 1 cup (250 mL) cold water and let stand 1 hour. Drain well. In a small bowl, combine wheat, parsley, green onions, garlic and mint. Peel, seed and chop 1 tomato. Add to mixture. Add oil, lemon juice, salt and pepper. Toss to combine, cover and refrigerate. At this point, salad will keep several days. To serve, place a spoonful for each person on a lettuce leaf and garnish with tomato wedges.
**Serves 6-8**

# Riviera Rice Salad

*This is delicious served with our cool, curried chicken.*

| | | |
|---|---|---|
| 3½ | cups boiling water | 875 mL |
| 2 | chicken bouillon envelopes or cubes | 2 |
| 1½ | cups converted rice | 375 mL |
| ½ | cup raisins | 125 mL |
| ½ | cup frozen or fresh peas | 125 mL |
| ½ | cup green onions, chopped | 125 mL |
| ¼ | cup Miracle Whip salad dressing | 50 mL |
| 2 | tablespoons chives, chopped | 30 mL |

## DRESSING

| | | |
|---|---|---|
| 3-4 | tablespoons wine vinegar | 45-60 mL |
| ⅔ | cup oil | 150 mL |
| ¾ | teaspoon salt | 4 mL |
| 1 | garlic clove, minced | 1 |
| 1 | teaspoon Dijon mustard | 5 mL |
| 1 | teaspoon tarragon | 5 mL |
| | Black pepper, freshly ground | |

To boiling water, add bouillon cubes and then rice. Reduce heat to simmer and cover tightly. After 10 minutes, add raisins, re-cover and cook for 10 minutes. Add fresh or frozen peas, re-cover and cook for 10 more minutes or until all the liquid is absorbed. Meanwhile, whisk together all ingredients for the dressing. When rice is done, remove from heat and add ½-¾ cup (125-175 mL) dressing. Stir well. Add green onions and Miracle Whip. If necessary, add more dressing to moisten. May be served warm or pressed into a salad mold and chilled. Garnish with chopped chives and/or cherry tomatoes.
**Serves 8-10**

# Mustard French Dressing on Asparagus or Green Beans

*A good basic vinaigrette to use on greens, too.*

| 1-1½ | pounds fresh asparagus or green beans | 500-750 | g |
|------|---------------------------------------|---------|---|

## DRESSING

| 1 | tablespoon onion, grated | 15 | mL |
|---|--------------------------|-----|----|
|   | Freshly ground pepper to taste | | |
| ½ | teaspoon salt | 2 | mL |
| 1 | tablespoon Dijon mustard | 15 | mL |
| 2 | tablespoons red wine vinegar | 30 | mL |
| ½ | cup olive oil | 125 | mL |
| ½ | teaspoon lemon juice | 2 | mL |

Steam vegetables, 4 minutes for asparagus, 5-8 minutes for green beans. Run under cold water to stop cooking, and drain well. When cool, place in a flat serving dish and refrigerate. In a separate bowl, whisk onion, salt, pepper, mustard and vinegar. Very slowly whisk in the oil. After oil is thoroughly mixed in, whisk in the lemon juice. Shortly before serving, spoon dressing over vegetables. Garnish with parsley or small lettuce leaves.

**Serves 4-6**

# Olé Salad

*A salad for your family reunion picnic!*

## DRESSING

| | | | |
|---|---|---|---|
| ½ | cup ketchup | 125 | mL |
| ½ | cup mayonnaise, regular or light | 125 | mL |

## SALAD

| | | | |
|---|---|---|---|
| 1 | pound lean hamburger | 500 | g |
| 1 | package taco seasoning mix | 1 | |
| 1 | head lettuce, shredded | 1 | |
| ½ | head red cabbage, shredded | ½ | |
| 1 | can (19 oz/540 mL) red kidney beans, drained and rinsed | 1 | |
| 1 | can (19 oz/540 mL) pitted black olives, sliced | 1 | |
| 1 | bunch green onions, chopped | 1 | |
| 1-2 | cups grated Cheddar cheese | 250-500 | mL |
| ¾ | cup celery, sliced | 175 | mL |
| 1 | tomato, quartered and chopped | 1 | |
| 1-1½ | cups corn chips, crushed | 250-375 | mL |

Mix ketchup and mayonnaise; refrigerate until ready to use. Pan-fry hamburger. Drain and add the taco seasoning. Mix well and continue frying until well cooked. Set aside. Layer a large salad bowl with the ingredients, ending with tomato. Garnish with crushed corn chips. Toss with dressing when ready to use.

**Serves 10-12**

# Kidney Bean Salad

*As simple as one, two, three.*

| | | |
|---|---|---|
| 1 | can (19 oz/540 mL) kidney beans, drained and rinsed | 1 |
| 3 | hard-boiled eggs, chopped | 3 |
| ½ | cup celery, diced | 125 mL |
| 2 | tablespoons onions or shallots, chopped | 30 mL |
| ¼ | cup mayonnaise, regular or light | 50 mL |
| 1 | teaspoon salt | 5 mL |
| ¼ | cup sweet pickle relish | 50 mL |
| 2 | tablespoons green pepper, chopped | 30 mL |

Mix, cover and chill.
**Serves 6-8**

# Broccoli Salad

*For buffet or summer luncheons.*

| | | |
|---|---|---|
| 3 | small bunches fresh broccoli | 3 |
| 1 | pound fresh mushrooms, sliced | 500 g |
| 2 | green onions, finely chopped | 2 |

**DRESSING**

| | | |
|---|---|---|
| ⅓ | cup sugar | 75 mL |
| 1 | teaspoon salt | 5 mL |
| 1 | teaspoon paprika | 5 mL |
| 1 | teaspoon celery seed | 5 mL |
| 1 | tablespoon onion powder | 15 mL |
| 1 | cup oil | 250 mL |
| ¼ | cup cider or wine vinegar | 50 mL |

Wash broccoli and break into florets. Mix with mushrooms and
onions in a sturdy plastic bag. Combine all ingredients for dressing
and pour over vegetables, coating all. Marinate in refrigerator for
2 hours, tossing occasionally. Drain off excess liquid before serving.
**Serves 12-16**

# Cauliflower and Broccoli Salad

*Moist, colourful and a hit with the whole family.*

| | | |
|---|---|---|
| 1 | cauliflower, raw and cut into florets | 1 |
| 3 | stalks broccoli, raw and cut into florets | 3 |
| 1 | red onion, thinly sliced | 1 |
| 1 | cup mayonnaise, regular or light | 250 mL |
| 1 | cup sour cream, regular or light | 250 mL |
| 1 | tablespoon vinegar | 15 mL |
| 1 | tablespoon sugar | 15 mL |
| | Salt and pepper to taste | |
| | Dash of Worcestershire sauce | |

Combine cauliflower, broccoli and onion. Mix remaining ingredients together and toss with the vegetables. Serve at once.
**Serves 8-10**

# Salad with Warm Brie

*Serve before or after the entrée and wait for the raves.*

| | | |
|---|---|---|
| 8 | small wedges of Brie cheese (or chèvre) | 8 |
| 1 | head Boston lettuce, washed and torn | 1 |
| 1 | head romaine lettuce, washed and torn | 1 |

**DRESSING**

| | | |
|---|---|---|
| ⅔ | cup olive oil | 150 mL |
| ⅓ | cup lemon juice | 75 mL |
| | Salt and freshly ground pepper to taste | |
| ½ | teaspoon dry mustard | 2 mL |

Mix dressing ingredients together; let stand at room temperature. Preheat oven to 350°F (180°C). Place salad into a bowl and toss with enough dressing to coat lettuce. Place cheese wedges on cookie sheet. Bake for about 2 minutes. Put salad on serving plates, place a wedge of warm cheese on each plate and serve immediately.
**Serves 8**

# Chinese Rice Salad

*Interesting with barbecued or cold meats.*

| 1 | cup converted long grain rice | 250 | mL |
| 1 | cup frozen peas, thawed, uncooked | 250 | mL |
| 1 | cup celery, finely chopped | 250 | mL |
| ½ | Spanish onion, finely chopped | ½ | |
| 1 | cup shrimp, cooked or canned | 250 | mL |
| 4 | ounces chow mein noodles | 125 | g |

## DRESSING

| ¼ | cup oil | 50 | mL |
| 2 | tablespoons vinegar | 30 | mL |
| 1½ | teaspoons soy sauce | 7 | mL |
| ½ | teaspoon curry powder | 2 | mL |
| ½ | teaspoon salt | 2 | mL |
| 1½ | teaspoons sugar | 7 | mL |
| ½ | teaspoon celery seed | 2 | mL |

Cook the rice according to directions; chill. This can be done a day
ahead. Add peas, celery, onion, and shrimp on the day of serving.
Put the dressing ingredients into a jar and shake well. Just before
serving, add dressing to salad a few spoonsful at a time until salad
appears moist enough. Add the noodles and toss.
**Serves 8**

# Spinach Salad and Five Ways to Dress It

## THE BASIC SALAD

| | | |
|---|---|---|
| 1-2 | bunches spinach, washed, dried and torn into bite-sized pieces | 1-2 |
| 1 | cup fresh mushrooms, thinly sliced | 250 mL |
| ½ | red onion, thinly sliced and separated into rings | ½ |
| 2 | eggs, hard-cooked and chopped | 2 |
| 6 | slices bacon, cooked crisp and crumbled | 6 |

Toss together and serve with one of the following dressings.
Serves 6-8

## 1. SWEET VINAIGRETTE

| | | |
|---|---|---|
| ½ | teaspoon salt | 2 mL |
| ¼ | teaspoon freshly ground pepper | 1 mL |
| 1-2 | tablespoons sugar or honey | 15-30 mL |
| 1 | teaspoon Dijon mustard or ¼ teaspoon/1 mL dry mustard | 5 mL |
| 2 | tablespoons wine vinegar or lemon juice | 30 mL |
| ½ | cup oil | 125 mL |

Whisk all ingredients, except oil, until dissolved. Add oil and whisk or shake in a covered jar. Toss with salad. This dressing will keep indefinitely in the refrigerator.
Makes ½ cup (125 mL)

## 2. HOT BACON DRESSING

Reserve the crumbled bacon for the dressing rather than the salad.

| | | |
|---|---|---|
| 6 | slices bacon, cooked crisp and crumbled | 6 |
| ¼ | cup hot bacon fat | 50 mL |
| ¼ | cup green onions, sliced | 50 mL |
| 1 | teaspoon tarragon | 5 mL |
| ¼ | cup sugar | 50 mL |
| ¼ | cup vinegar | 50 mL |
| ¼ | cup water | 50 mL |
| 2 | teaspoons cornstarch dissolved in | 10 mL |
| | 1 tablespoon (15 mL) water | |
| | Salt and pepper to taste | |

In a sauce pan, over medium heat, combine bacon fat, sugar, vinegar, water, tarragon and green onions. Stir in cornstarch and water mixture; continue stirring until dressing thickens. Add crumbled bacon bits and season to taste. Pour dressing into gravy boat and ladle over individual salad servings.
**Makes about ¾ cup (175 mL)**

## 3. TANGY CHUTNEY DRESSING

Beansprouts and grated Swiss cheese may be added to the Basic Salad.

| | | |
|---|---|---|
| ¼ | cup wine vinegar | 50 mL |
| ¼ | cup Major Grey's chutney | 50 mL |
| 1 | garlic clove | 1 |
| 2 | tablespoons (scant) Dijon or hot mustard | 30 mL |
| 1 | tablespoon sugar | 15 mL |
| ⅓-½ | cup oil | 75-125 mL |
| | Salt and white pepper to taste | |

Combine vinegar, chutney, garlic, mustard and sugar in a food processor or blender and process until smooth. Add oil, drop by drop, and then in a steady stream until thick. Season to taste. Refrigerate.
**Makes about 1 cup (250 mL)**

## 4. MAPLE VINAIGRETTE

Try either of these maple dressings on a mixture of fresh spinach leaves (baby spinach is especially nice), orange segments, sliced red onion and toasted sunflower seeds or pine nuts.

| | | | |
|---|---|---|---|
| ¼ | cup balsamic or raspberry vinegar | 50 | mL |
| ¼ | cup olive oil | 50 | mL |
| 1 | teaspoon Dijon mustard | 5 | mL |
| 2-4 | tablespoons maple syrup | 30-60 | mL |
| | Salt and pepper to taste | | |

Whisk dressing ingredients together or shake together in a jar. Toss salad with enough dressing to coat the leaves.

**Makes about ¾ cup (175 mL)**

## 5. CREAMY MAPLE VINAIGRETTE

Whisk ¼ cup (50 mL) low-fat sour cream, yogourt or mayonnaise with Maple Vinaigrette and toss with salad at serving time.

**Makes about 1 cup (250 mL)**

# A Friend's Salad Dressing

| ½ | cup oil | 125 | mL |
|---|---|---|---|
| 1 | teaspoon salt | 5 | mL |
| 1 | teaspoon Worcestershire sauce | 5 | mL |
| 1 | teaspoon horseradish | 5 | mL |
| 1 | garlic clove, minced | 1 | |
| 3 | tablespoons vinegar, wine or white | 45 | mL |
| | Dash of Tabasco sauce | | |
| | Ground pepper to taste | | |

Combine all of the above ingredients. Shake well. Allow to stand several hours before serving.

**Makes ¾ cup (175 mL)**

# Creamy Salad Dressing

*Good with Boston lettuce, bean sprouts, scallions and mushrooms.*

| | | |
|---|---|---|
| 1 | teaspoon coarse salt | 5 mL |
| ¼ | teaspoon sugar | 1 mL |
| ½ | teaspoon black pepper | 2 mL |
| ½ | teaspoon white pepper | 2 mL |
| ½ | teaspoon dry mustard | 2 mL |
| 1 | teaspoon Dijon mustard | 5 mL |
| 1 | garlic clove, minced | 1 |
| 1 | teaspoon lemon juice | 5 mL |
| 2 | tablespoons tarragon or balsamic vinegar | 30 mL |
| 2 | tablespoons olive oil | 30 mL |
| ⅔ | cup vegetable oil | 150 mL |
| ½ | cup light cream | 125 mL |
| 1 | raw egg | 1 |

Place ingredients in jar and shake well or blend in blender. Chill.
Keeps in refrigerator for 2-3 days.

**Makes 1½ cups (375 mL)**

# Casual Dining
## Brunch, Lunch and Supper

# Crab and Asparagus Strata

*A super brunch, lunch or late-night repast!*

| | | | |
|---|---|---|---|
| 5 | cups bread, cubed | 1.25 | L |
| 1 | can (5 oz/142 g) crab, drained and flaked | 1 | |
| ½ | pound fresh asparagus, 1-inch (2.5 cm) lengths, steamed (or 1 can [10 oz/284 mL] green asparagus pieces, drained) | 250 | g |
| 1 | can (10 oz/284 mL) white asparagus, drained | 1 | |
| 2 | cups Cheddar cheese, shredded | 500 | mL |
| 6 | large eggs | 6 | |
| 3 | cups milk | 750 | mL |
| 1 | small onion, finely chopped | 1 | |
| ½ | teaspoon salt | 2 | mL |
| 1 | teaspoon dry mustard | 5 | mL |

Preheat oven to 350°F (180°C). Butter a 6-cup (1.5-L) straight-sided dish or a large lasagne pan. Layer ⅓ each of bread, crab, asparagus and cheese. Repeat to make 3 layers. Beat eggs, milk, onion, salt and mustard until blended. Pour over layers. Cover and refrigerate at least 3 hours, preferably overnight. Bake, covered with foil, for 1 hour. Remove foil and bake 10 minutes longer or until puffed and golden. Serve immediately.

**VARIATIONS:**

1. Substitute 1½ cups (375 mL) cubed ham for crab.
2. Substitute 1½ cups (375 mL) cubed cooked chicken for crab, and broccoli for asparagus.

**Serves 8**

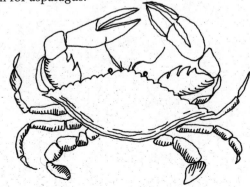

# Hot Crab Avocado

*Nice twist on an old theme!*

| | | |
|---|---|---|
| 1 | can (6 oz/170 g) crabmeat, drained and cartilage removed | 1 |
| ⅓ | cup celery, chopped | 75 mL |
| 2 | tablespoons pimento, chopped | 30 mL |
| 3 | hard-boiled eggs, chopped (optional) | 3 |
| 1 | tablespoon onion, chopped | 15 mL |
| ½ | teaspoon salt | 2 mL |
| ½ | cup mayonnaise, regular or light | 125 mL |
| 3 | large or 4 medium ripe avocados | 3 |
| | Lemon juice | |
| | Salt | |
| 3 | tablespoons dry bread crumbs | 45 mL |
| 1 | teaspoon butter, melted | 5 mL |
| 2 | tablespoons slivered almonds | 30 mL |

Preheat oven to 400°F (200°C). Mix crabmeat, celery, pimento, eggs, onion, salt and mayonnaise. Cut unpeeled avocados in half length-wise, brush with lemon juice and sprinkle with salt. Fill avocado halves with crabmeat mixture. Toss bread crumbs with melted butter and spoon over avocados. Place in a shallow baking dish and bake, uncovered, for 10 minutes; sprinkle almonds over the top. Bake 5 minutes longer or until filling is hot and bubbly. Serve at once.
**Serves 6-8**

# Curried Eggs

*Great family meal or lunch.*

| | | | |
|---|---|---:|---|
| 3 | onions, sliced | 3 | |
| ½ | cup butter | 125 | mL |
| ¼ | cup flour | 50 | mL |
| ¼ | teaspoon salt | 1 | mL |
| 2 | tablespoons curry powder | 30 | mL |
| 2 | cups chicken stock or broth | 500 | mL |
| 12 | small, hard-boiled eggs | 12 | |
| 2-3 | cups cooked rice | 500-750 | mL |
| ¼ | cup raisins | 50 | mL |
| ¼ | cup almonds, toasted | 50 | mL |

Sauté onions in ¼ cup (50 mL) butter until nicely browned; remove.
Melt ¼ cup (50 mL) butter and stir in flour and salt. When well
blended, add curry powder and the stock. Cook, stirring until thick
and smooth. Add onions and shelled eggs. Cover and simmer for
30 minutes. On a platter make a ring of rice; cut eggs in half and
place in centre. Pour sauce around them. Garnish with raisins,
almonds and cooked asparagus or broccoli.
**Serves 4-6**

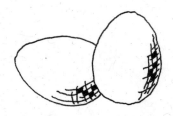

# Easy, Elegant Lunch

*Really easy!*

| | | |
|---|---|---|
| 1 | cup fresh mushrooms, sliced | 250 mL |
| 2 | tablespoons butter | 30 mL |
| 2 | tablespoons flour | 30 mL |
| ½ | cup 10% cream, or milk | 125 mL |
| 1 | can (10 oz/284 mL) cream of mushroom soup | 1 |
| ⅓ | cup white wine | 75 mL |
| 3 | tablespoons Parmesan cheese, grated | 45 mL |
| 2 | packages (each 7 oz/200 g) frozen cooked shrimp (or 2½ cups/625 mL cooked chicken or ham) | 2 |
| 1 | can (15 oz/426 mL) artichoke hearts, drained and halved | 1 |
| ¼ | cup slivered almonds, toasted | 50 mL |
| ¼ | cup pimento | 50 mL |
| 6 | patty shells or toast points | 6 |

In saucepan, cook mushrooms in butter and push to one side. Add flour to make a roux. Cook a minute, then add cream. Cook over low heat until thickened, stirring constantly. Blend in soup, wine and cheese. Add shrimp and artichokes; heat through. Stir gently. Serve from a chafing dish, garnished with almonds and pimentos, or pour over patty shells or toast points.

**Serves 6**

# Chicken and Asparagus Casserole

*Simple, quick luncheon, brunch or supper dish.*

| | | |
|---|---|---|
| 3 | whole chicken breasts | 3 |
| ¾ | pound fresh mushrooms, sliced | 375 g |
| 1 | garlic clove, minced | 1 |
| 3 | tablespoons butter | 45 mL |
| 1 | pound fresh asparagus, cut into | 500 g |
| | 1-inch (2.5-cm) pieces and cooked | |
| 2 | cans (each 10 oz/284 mL) cream of | 2 |
| | chicken soup | |
| | Dash of cayenne | |
| ½ | cup mayonnaise | 125 mL |
| ¼ | cup dry vermouth | 50 mL |
| | Buttered bread crumbs | |

Preheat oven to 350°F (180°C). Simmer chicken in water, just enough
to cover, for 20 minutes. Remove chicken from bones, separating
each into thirds or larger pieces. Sauté mushrooms and garlic in
butter. In a buttered 9" × 13" (3.5 L) baking dish, layer chicken,
asparagus and mushrooms. Combine soup, cayenne, mayonnaise
and vermouth; pour over chicken. Top with buttered bread crumbs
and bake, uncovered, for 45 minutes. If fresh asparagus is unavailable,
use 2 packages (each 10 oz/284 mL) frozen asparagus, cooked.
**Serves 8**

**VARIATION:** Try 2 (each 15 oz/426 mL) cans artichoke hearts,
drained and halved, instead of asparagus.

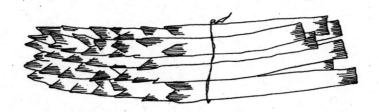

# Asparagus Cheese Soufflé Roll

| | | |
|---|---|---|
| ⅓ | cup butter | 75 mL |
| ⅓ | cup flour | 75 mL |
| ½ | teaspoon salt | 2 mL |
| 1¼ | cups milk | 300 mL |
| ½ | cup Cheddar cheese, grated | 125 mL |
| 7 | eggs, separated | 7 |
| ¼ | teaspoon cream of tartar | 1 mL |
| 2 | tablespoons butter | 30 mL |
| 1 | small onion, finely chopped | 1 |
| ⅔ | cup almonds, sliced | 150 mL |
| 1 | tablespoon flour | 15 mL |
| 1 | teaspoon salt | 5 mL |
| ½ | teaspoon nutmeg | 2 mL |
| | Pepper, freshly ground | |
| 1 | pound asparagus, cooked, drained and chopped | 500 g |
| 8 | ounces Swiss cheese, grated | 250 g |
| 1 | cup sour cream, regular or light | 250 mL |
| 1 | tablespoon Dijon mustard | 15 mL |

Preheat oven to 350°F (180°C). Line a 15" × 10" (2 L) jelly roll pan with foil and grease well. Melt butter in a large saucepan; stir in flour and salt until smooth. Gradually add milk; bring to a boil while stirring. Simmer until thick. Blend in Cheddar cheese and lightly beaten egg yolks. Remove from heat. Beat egg whites with cream of tartar until soft peaks form. Fold ⅓ whites into the cheese mixture; carefully fold in the remaining whites. Turn into the prepared pan. Bake for 15-20 minutes until puffed and firm to the touch.

While the soufflé roll is baking, sauté the onions and almonds in 2 tablespoons (30 mL) butter. Sprinkle with 1 tablespoon (15 mL) flour; stir to blend. Add seasonings and asparagus; stir for five minutes or until most of the moisture has evaporated. Remove from heat.

With a metal spatula, loosen the edges of the soufflé roll. Turn out onto a tea towel and remove the foil gently. Spread asparagus mixture gently on top. Sprinkle with cheese. Roll up, jelly roll fashion; place on a serving dish. Let stand a few minutes in a warm oven. Mix sour cream and mustard and serve over the soufflé roll.

**Serves 6**

# Quizza

*Lunch, snack, appetizer.*

| | | |
|---|---|---|
| 5 | eggs | 5 |
| 1 | cup creamed cottage cheese, small curd | 250 mL |
| ½ | package (1½ oz/43 g) spaghetti sauce with mushrooms mix | ½ |
| 1 | garlic clove, minced | 1 |
| ½ | teaspoon oregano, dried | 2 mL |
| ½ | teaspoon basil, dried | 2 mL |
| 1 | tablespoon flour | 15 mL |
| 1 | cup Monterey Jack cheese, shredded | 250 mL |
| 1 | cup Mozzarella cheese, shredded | 250 mL |
| ¼ | cup butter, melted | 50 mL |
| ½ | cup canned mushrooms, sliced and drained | 125 mL |
| ½ | green pepper, diced | ½ |
| ⅓ | cup ripe olives, sliced | 75 mL |
| ¼ | cup Parmesan cheese, grated | 50 mL |

Preheat oven to 400°F (200°C). Mix the first 7 ingredients in a blender or food processor. Stir in cheese, butter and mushrooms. Pour into a greased and floured 8" (2 L) square pan. Sprinkle with green pepper and olives. Top with Parmesan cheese. Bake, uncovered, for 15 minutes. Reduce heat to 350°F (180°C) and bake 25 to 35 minutes longer. Cut into 1-inch (2.5-cm) squares and serve warm or cold. Recipe can be doubled easily for a 9" × 13" (3.5 L) rectangular pan.

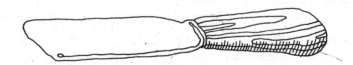

# San Francisco Seafood Quiche

| 2 | 8" (2 L) pie shells | 2 | |
|---|---|---|---|
| 1 | can (4 oz/113 g) king crab meat | 1 | |
| 1 | can (4 oz/113 g) shrimp | 1 | |
| 8 | ounces natural Swiss cheese, chopped | 250 | g |
| ½ | cup celery, finely chopped | 125 | mL |
| ½ | cup scallions, finely chopped | 125 | mL |
| 1 | cup mayonnaise | 250 | mL |
| 2 | tablespoons flour | 30 | mL |
| 1 | cup dry white wine | 250 | mL |
| 4 | eggs, slightly beaten | 4 | |

Preheat oven to 350°F (180°C). Combine crab, shrimp, cheese, celery and scallions. Divide mixture between pie shells. Combine mayonnaise, flour, wine and eggs. Mix well; divide sauce between pie shells, covering seafood. Bake pies for 35-40 minutes or until knife comes out clean. If making a day ahead, cool, cover with plastic wrap and refrigerate until needed. Bring to room temperature and reheat at 300°F (150°C) for 15 minutes.

**Serves 6-8**

# Cottage Cheese Pancakes

*Light and tasty—may well become an old standby!*

| 4 | eggs, slightly beaten | 4 | |
|---|---|---|---|
| 1 | cup cottage cheese | 250 | mL |
| ½ | cup flour | 125 | mL |
| 6 | tablespoons butter, melted | 90 | mL |

Mix all ingredients in a blender or food processor. Add a little milk if the batter seems too thick. Cook spoonfuls of batter on a hot griddle or fry pan until brown on the bottom. Turn and brown on the other side. Serve while hot.

**Serves 4**

# Frittata Quiche

*No crust to add calories!*

| | | |
|---|---|---|
| ¾ | cup green pepper, chopped | 175 mL |
| 1½ | cups mushrooms, sliced | 375 mL |
| 1½ | cups zucchini, diced | 375 mL |
| ¾ | cup onion, chopped | 175 mL |
| 1 | garlic clove, minced | 1 |
| 1 | tablespoon oil | 15 mL |
| 6 | eggs, beaten | 6 |
| ¼ | cup 10% cream or milk | 50 mL |
| ½ | pound cream cheese, diced (optional) | 250 g |
| 1½ | cups Cheddar cheese, shredded | 375 mL |
| 2 | cups bread cubes | 500 mL |
| 1 | teaspoon salt | 5 mL |
| ¼ | teaspoon pepper | 1 mL |

Preheat oven to 350°F (180°C). Sauté all vegetables in oil until crisp tender. Cool slightly. Meanwhile, beat eggs with cream or milk; add cheeses, bread, salt, pepper and vegetables. Mix well. Pour into a greased 10" (3 L) springform pan. Bake for 1 hour or until set in the centre. Cool 5 minutes before serving.

**Serves 8**

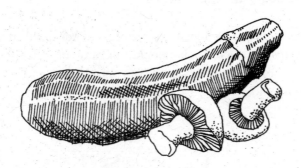

# Cheese Pie

*Serve for lunch or brunch as an alternative for quiche.*

## CRUST

| | | | |
|---|---|---|---|
| ¾ | cup flour | 175 | mL |
| ¾ | cup sharp Cheddar cheese, grated | 175 | mL |
| ½ | teaspoon dry mustard | 2 | mL |
| ½ | teaspoon salt | 2 | mL |
| ¼ | cup butter, melted | 50 | mL |

## FILLING

| | | | |
|---|---|---|---|
| 1 | tablespoon butter | 15 | mL |
| 1 | medium onion, thinly sliced | 1 | |
| 6 | mushrooms, finely chopped | 6 | |
| ⅔ | cup Cheddar cheese, grated | 150 | mL |
| 1 | cup hot, cooked egg noodles | 250 | mL |
| | Salt and pepper to taste | | |
| 2 | eggs, well beaten | 2 | |
| ¾ | cup hot milk | 175 | mL |

Preheat oven to 325°F (160°C). To prepare crust, mix together flour, Cheddar, mustard, salt and butter. Use more butter if needed. Press firmly into a 9" (1 L) pie plate. Lightly sauté onions and mushrooms in butter until browned. Pour over crust. Alternate layers of noodles and Cheddar, dusting with salt and pepper. Add beaten eggs. Slowly pour in the hot milk. Bake for 50 minutes.

**Serves 6**

# Sweet Red Pepper Tart

*The hit of the brunch table!*

| | | | |
|---|---|---|---|
| 1 | 10-inch (1.2-L) pie crust | 1 | |
| 1 | tablespoon Dijon mustard | 15 | mL |
| 3 | tablespoons unsalted butter | 45 | mL |
| 2 | onions, finely chopped | 2 | |
| 1 | garlic clove, minced | 1 | |
| 3 | large sweet red peppers, diced | 3 | |
| 1 | green pepper, diced | 1 | |
| 1 | cup Swiss cheese, grated | 250 | mL |
| 2 | tablespoons fresh parsley or basil, chopped | 30 | mL |
| 4 | eggs | 4 | |
| 1½ | cups 18% cream or 2% evaporated milk | 375 | mL |
| 1 | teaspoon salt | 5 | mL |
| ¼ | teaspoon pepper, freshly ground | 1 | mL |
| | Pinch of nutmeg | | |
| | Pinch of cayenne pepper | | |

Preheat oven to 450°F (230°C). Bake pie shell for 10 minutes. Remove. Reduce heat to 350°F (180°C). Brush bottom of pie shell with mustard. In a skillet, melt butter and sauté onions and garlic over medium heat until tender, about 10 minutes. Add peppers and cook 6 to 8 minutes longer, until they are tender. Cool slightly. Spread vegetable mixture on the bottom of the crust and sprinkle cheese on top. Sprinkle with basil or parsley. Beat eggs with cream or milk. Add salt, nutmeg, pepper and cayenne. Pour over peppers. Bake for 30 to 40 minutes or until top is golden brown and slightly puffy. Cool 10 minutes before serving.

**Serves 8**

# My Aunt Ev's French-Style Picnic Pie

*A very elegant picnic or Christmas tortière!*

| | | | |
|---|---|---|---|
| 2 | tablespoons butter | 30 | mL |
| 1 | medium onion, chopped | 1 | |
| 2 | garlic cloves, minced | 2 | |
| ½ | cup dry white wine | 125 | mL |
| 1 | pound cooked turkey, ground | 500 | g |
| 1 | pound cooked ground veal or | 500 | g |
| | 1 pound cooked bulk pork sausage, partially drained | | |
| 1 | pound cooked ham, ground | 500 | g |
| ½ | cup homemade dry bread crumbs | 125 | mL |
| ¼ | cup parsley, chopped | 50 | mL |
| 1 | egg | 1 | |
| ½ | teaspoon each salt, thyme and dry mustard | 2 | mL |
| ¼ | teaspoon ground allspice | 1 | mL |
| ¼ | teaspoon black pepper | 1 | mL |
| 1 | egg white, beaten with 1 teaspoon (5 mL) water | 1 | |
| | A double batch of your favourite pastry | | |

Preheat oven to 375°F (190°C). Melt butter in fry pan, add onion and cook until limp. Stir in garlic and wine. Bring to boil and cook, stirring until most of the liquid is evaporated. Combine onion mixture with turkey, veal (or pork), ham, crumbs, parsley, egg, salt, thyme, mustard, allspice and pepper. Set aside. Prepare pastry. Roll out larger portion on a lightly floured board; fit into a 10-inch (3-L) springform pan. Trim edge so pastry overhangs ½ inch (1 cm). Pat meat mixture evenly into crust. Roll out remaining pastry and place over filling. Moisten edges and flute together to seal. Cut a small vent in centre. Brush evenly with egg white/water mixture. Bake on lowest rack for approximately 45 minutes or until well browned. To serve, cool to room temperature or chill and remove sides of pan.
**Serves 8-10**

# Mexican Ground Beef

*Quick and tasty!*

| | | | |
|---|---|---|---|
| 6 | slices bacon | 6 | |
| 1 | cup onions, chopped | 250 | mL |
| ½ | cup green pepper, chopped | 125 | mL |
| 2 | garlic cloves, minced | 2 | |
| 1½ | pounds ground beef | 750 | g |
| 1 | can (28 oz/796 mL) tomatoes, chopped with juice | 1 | |
| | Salt and pepper to taste | | |
| 1 | tablespoon chili powder | 15 | mL |
| 1 | cup kernel corn | 250 | mL |
| 1 | cup kidney beans, rinsed and drained | 250 | mL |
| 2 | cups potatoes, peeled and diced | 500 | mL |

Fry bacon until crisp. Drain and set aside. Sauté onion, green pepper and garlic in bacon drippings. Add ground beef and cook until browned. Lower heat and add tomatoes and juice, salt, pepper, chili powder, corn, beans and potatoes. Cook 45 minutes or until potatoes are tender. When ready to serve, crumble bacon over top.
**Serves 6**

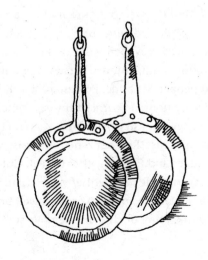

# Overnight Beef Casserole

*Kids love this!*

| | | | |
|---|---|---|---|
| 1 | cup shell macaroni | 250 | mL |
| 2 | pounds ground beef | 1 | kg |
| 1 | green pepper, diced | 1 | |
| 3 | onions, minced | 3 | |
| 3 | garlic cloves, minced | 3 | |
| 2 | cans (each 14 oz/398 mL) tomato sauce | 2 | |
| 1 | can (7 oz/199 mL) corn niblets | 1 | |
| 1 | can (10 oz/284 mL) mushrooms | 1 | |
| 1 | cup Cheddar cheese, grated | 250 | mL |
| 1 | tablespoon brown sugar | 15 | mL |
| 1 | teaspoon chili powder | 5 | mL |
| 1 | tablespoon Worcestershire sauce | 15 | mL |
| 1 | teaspoon salt | 5 | mL |
| ¼ | teaspoon pepper | 1 | mL |
| ½ | cup sherry | 125 | mL |

Cook macaroni and cool. Sauté meat with green pepper, onions and garlic. In a casserole, combine the rest of the ingredients. Add macaroni and meat mixture. Chill overnight. Preheat oven to 350°F (180°C). Bake for 1 hour or until bubbly and hot.
**Serves 10**

# The Mississauga Evacuation Special

*On November 11, 1979, the derailment and subsequent explosion of a train carrying a cargo of deadly chlorine gas prompted the evacuation of over a quarter of a million people from the city of Mississauga, Ontario, just west of Toronto. This emptying of a city, which took place swiftly and without injury or loss of life, was the largest in the history of North America. Many families who, for almost a week, took refuge with friends and relatives in surrounding areas made this meal famous.*

| 8-12 | onions, peeled and chopped in big chunks | 8-12 | |
| 4 | tablespoons oil | 60 | mL |
| 1 | cup ketchup | 250 | mL |
| | Worcestershire sauce to taste | | |
| 1 | cup water | 250 | mL |
| 2 | pounds ground beef | 1 | kg |
| 2 | garlic cloves, minced | 2 | |
| | Salt and pepper to taste | | |
| 2 | cans (each 28 oz/796 mL) Heinz spaghetti* | 2 | |
| ½-1 | pound Cheddar cheese, grated | 250-500 | g |

Preheat oven to 350°F (180°C). In a large, enamelled, cast-iron Dutch oven, sauté onions in oil until translucent but not brown. Add ketchup, Worcestershire sauce and water. Simmer until onions are mushy and mixture is soupy. This is your first layer. While the onions are bubbling away, brown the meat in a frying pan with garlic and seasonings. Drain fat and layer meat on top of onions to make second layer. Cover meat with spaghetti. Cover spaghetti with cheese. Bake for 1 hour. Serve with garlic bread and a crisp green salad.
**Serves a crowd**

**\*TIP:** Canned spaghetti can be replaced with leftover pasta in tomato sauce (any shape will do).

# Easy Beer Stew

*Hearty, with lots of gravy for dipping!*

| | | | |
|---|---|---|---|
| 2 | pounds stewing beef, cubed | 1 | kg |
| 3-4 | onions, quartered | 3-4 | |
| 1 | large can (19 oz/540 mL) tomato soup | 1 | |
| 1 | can beer | 1 | |
| 4 | heaping tablespoons Bisto powdered gravy browner (or 5 tablespoons/75 mL Bovril bouillon concentrate) | 65 | mL |
| | Lots of freshly ground pepper | | |
| 6 | medium-sized potatoes, cut into chunks | 6 | |
| 6-8 | carrots, cut into chunks | 6-8 | |

Preheat oven to 350°F (180°C). Arrange uncooked beef cubes and onions in a large casserole. Add pepper, tomato soup, beer and Bisto. Mix gently and cover tightly with aluminum foil. Bake for 2 hours. Remove from oven; add potatoes and carrots. Cover and return to oven for 1 more hour, or until vegetables are cooked.
**Serves 6-8**

**TIP:** Try adding chopped celery, parsnip, turnip or canned tomatoes and fresh herbs, but then it won't be quite so easy!

# Sweet and Sour Chicken Wings

*Recipe can be doubled!*

| | | | |
|---|---|---|---|
| 2 | pounds chicken wings | 1 | kg |
| | Seasoned flour | | |
| 2 | tablespoons oil | 30 | mL |
| 1 | small onion, chopped | 1 | |
| ⅔ | cup orange juice | 150 | mL |
| ⅓ | cup ketchup | 75 | mL |
| 1 | tablespoon brown sugar | 15 | mL |
| 1 | teaspoon soy sauce | 5 | mL |
| ¼ | teaspoon ground ginger | 1 | mL |

Preheat oven to 350°F (180°C). Snip off wing tips and discard.
Dredge wings in flour and brown in hot fat. Lift wings into casserole.
Add remaining ingredients to frying pan and bring to a boil. Stir
well. Pour over wings, cover and bake for ½ hour. Turn and bake
½ hour longer.

**Serves 4-6**

**TIP:** This sauce is also good with meat balls.

# Barbecued Chicken Wings

*This sauce is also excellent for spareribs.*

| 12 | chicken wings | 12 | |
|----|---------------|-----|-----|
| ½ | cup honey or maple syrup | 125 | mL |
| ½ | cup ketchup | 125 | mL |
| ½ | cup barbecue sauce | 125 | mL |
| 4 | tablespoons soy sauce | 60 | mL |

Preheat oven to 350°F (180°C). Place chicken wings on cookie sheet and broil lightly on each side until skin is crisp. Drain on paper towel. Mix together remaining ingredients in saucepan and simmer for 5 minutes. Place chicken wings in covered Dutch oven, cover with sauce, and bake for 1 hour. Serve with rice as a family dinner. If they are to be served as hors d'oeuvres, you may wish to divide wings at joints, discarding the tip portion.

**Serves 4**

# Barbecued Spareribs

| | | | |
|---|---|---|---|
| 2 | pounds pork ribs | 1 | kg |
| 2 | tablespoons oil | 30 | mL |
| 2 | cups celery, chopped | 500 | mL |
| 1 | medium onion, chopped | 1 | |
| ¾ | cup ketchup | 175 | mL |
| ¼ | cup vinegar | 50 | mL |
| ½ | cup brown sugar | 125 | mL |
| 1 | cup water | 250 | mL |
| | Salt and pepper to taste | | |

Preheat oven to 350°F (180°C). Place ribs in pan and add enough water to cover the ribs. Cover and cook for two hours. Drain off liquid and fat. About 15 minutes before ribs are ready, heat oil in frying pan and sauté onions and celery until tender. Add remaining ingredients, season to taste and simmer for 15 minutes. Add to ribs and bake one more hour.

**Serves 4-6**

# Pepper Pocket Panzarotti

*Hungry man's snack!*

| 2 | loaves frozen bread dough, defrosted | 2 | |
| 20 | slices Genoa salami or 2 sticks pepperoni, sliced | 20 | |
| 20 | slices mild Provolone cheese | 20 | |
| 4-6 | green peppers, thinly sliced | 4-6 | |
| 2 | tablespoons olive oil | 30 | mL |

Preheat oven to 350°F (180°C). Roll out each loaf of defrosted dough onto a floured board. Shape into a rectangle, approximately 8" × 14" (20 cm × 35 cm). Sauté peppers in olive oil. Layer salami on dough. Cover with Provolone and peppers, then cover with the second rectangle. Pinch edges to make a package. Paint the top with a pastry brush dipped in the oil residue left from the peppers. If desired, cut "package" in half for easier handling. Place on a cookie sheet and bake for 35 minutes. Slice to desired size. This can be made a day ahead. Cover and refrigerate until you are ready to bake it.

**Serves 8-10 as a snack or 25 as an appetizer**

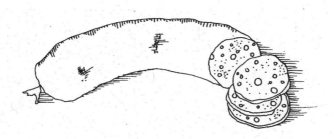

# Fettuccine with Asparagus

*Substitute peas, broccoli, smoked salmon, shrimps, etc., for asparagus.*

| | | | |
|---|---|---|---|
| 1 | pound fettuccine, egg or spinach noodles | 500 | g |
| 1 | pound asparagus, cut into 1-inch (2.5-cm) pieces and cooked | 500 | g |
| ½ | cup butter, softened | 125 | mL |
| ½ | cup whipping cream | 125 | mL |
| 3 | egg yolks | 3 | |
| 1 | cup Parmesan cheese, freshly grated | 250 | mL |
| 2 | tablespoons green onions, finely chopped | 30 | mL |
| 3 | tablespoons butter | 45 | mL |
| | Salt and pepper to taste | | |

Put a large pot of salted water on to boil. Warm a serving dish in the oven. Cream ½ cup (125 mL) butter until light and fluffy. Gradually beat in cream and egg yolks. Beat in cheese a few spoonfuls at a time. Reserve. Melt 3 tablespoons (45 mL) butter in a skillet and gently cook green onions. Add asparagus and roll in butter and onion; cook briefly. Season with salt and pepper. Keep warm over low heat. Boil fettuccine until al dente. Drain and transfer to warm serving dish. Toss with butter and cheese mixture. Add asparagus and green onions. Toss and season with salt and pepper to taste. Serve immediately with additional grated Parmesan.

**Serves 4-6**

# Linguine al Limone

*Could be the basis for a very elegant but simple lunch.*

| | | |
|---|---|---|
| 2 | lemons | 2 |
| 1 | pound linguine or spaghetti, preferably fresh | 500 g |
| 1 | cup whipping cream | 250 mL |
| ¼ | cup brandy | 50 mL |
| ¾ | cup Parmesan cheese, freshly grated | 175 mL |
| 2 | tablespoons butter | 30 mL |
| | Freshly ground pepper to taste | |

Carefully remove a thin layer of rind from lemons, using a vegetable peeler. Mince very finely. There will be about 2 tablespoons (30 mL). Set aside. Remove all of the white pith from lemons, and section flesh, discarding membranes and seeds. Set aside. Cook linguine in lots of boiling salted water until al dente. Meanwhile, in a small heavy saucepan over low heat, bring cream, brandy and lemon pulp to a boil. Boil gently for 7-8 minutes until slightly reduced. Place drained linguine in a large, warm bowl and toss with butter. Add sauce and toss to combine. Add cheese and toss again. Serve immediately with reserved lemon zest.

**Serves 6**

# Pasta con Verdura

*A quick treat for pasta lovers.*

| | | |
|---|---|---|
| 1 | cup small broccoli florets | 250 mL |
| 1 | small zucchini, sliced | 1 |
| 1 | small, sweet red pepper, cut in strips | 1 |
| ½ | cup snow peas | 125 mL |
| ¼ | cup butter, unsalted preferably | 50 mL |
| 1 | cup 10% cream, warmed | 250 mL |
| | freshly ground black pepper | |
| 1 | pound spaghetti, cooked and drained | 500 g |
| | Parmesan cheese, grated | |

In a large skillet, sauté broccoli, zucchini, red pepper and snow peas
in butter until crisp tender. Add cream and black pepper. Cook briefly
until slightly reduced. Mix with pasta and sprinkle with Parmesan.
Serve immediately.

**Serves 4**

# Elegant Entrées

## Fish, Meat and Poultry

# Grouper in Tomato Sauce

*Gorgeous!*

| | | | |
|---|---|---|---|
| 3 | tablespoons olive oil | 45 | mL |
| ½ | pound tomatoes, cut up or canned | 250 | g |
| 2 | bay leaves | 2 | |
| ½ | teaspoon marjoram | 2 | mL |
| 3 | pounds grouper, fillets or steaks | 1500 | g |
| | Salt and freshly ground pepper to taste | | |
| 2 | tablespoons butter, softened | 30 | mL |
| 1 | tablespoon flour | 15 | mL |
| 3 | tablespoons Italian parsley, chopped | 45 | mL |

Preheat oven to 400°F (200°C). Put the olive oil, tomato chunks, bay leaves and marjoram into a large casserole. Season grouper with salt and pepper and place into casserole. Turn to coat well. Bake for 20 minutes, basting once with the sauce. Remove from oven and keep hot on a platter. Strain the sauce through a sieve into a small saucepan. Press hard to remove as much liquid as possible. Bring to a simmer. Mix the butter and flour together and stir into sauce. Cook for 4-5 minutes. Adjust seasoning. Pour over grouper, sprinkle with parsley and serve at once.
**Serves 6**

# Poached Salmon in Rosé Wine

*This is quite a simple procedure that produces spectacular results! It can be used for any other type of fish such as Red Snapper, etc.*

| | | |
|---|---|---|
| 1 | 4-5 pound (2-2.5 kg) whole, fresh Cohoe salmon | 1 |
| ¼ | cup shallots, chopped | 50 mL |
| 1 | stalk celery with leaves, cut up | 1 |
| 1 | carrot, cut up | 1 |
| 1 | bunch of parsley | 1 |
| 1 | teaspoon salt | 5 mL |
| 4 | cups water | 1 L |
| 2½ | cups rosé wine | 625 mL |
| 2 | lemons, cut in wedges | 2 |

Combine shallots, celery, carrot, four sprigs of parsley, salt and water in a saucepan. Bring to a boil, reduce heat and simmer, uncovered, for 20 minutes. Pour this stock into a fish poacher or large roasting pan. Add the rosé wine. Wash the fish inside and out. Place on a rack and into the pan. If the fish is not at least half covered by the bouillon, add up to one cup (250 mL) of extra water and then more wine as necessary. Bring the stock just under the point of boiling so that the water appears to shiver rather than bubble. If you cook the fish faster than this, the fish will tend to fall apart. Poach, covered, for 35 minutes or just until the fish flakes easily with a fork. Carefully lift the rack with the fish on it from the pan and remove any bits of celery, etc., that may adhere to its surface. Place the fish on a platter; garnish with lemon wedges and the rest of the parsley. Serve with Hollandaise sauce or our Green Sauce for Salmon (p. 195). **Serves 10**

# Snow Peas and Shrimp

*Tasty last-minute meal.*

| | | | |
|---|---|---|---|
| 1½ | teaspoons cornstarch | 7 | mL |
| ¼ | teaspoon ground ginger (or 1 teaspoon/ 5 mL fresh ginger, grated) | 1 | mL |
| 1½ | tablespoons soy sauce | 25 | mL |
| 2 | tablespoons dry sherry | 30 | mL |
| ½ | cup chicken broth | 125 | mL |
| 3 | tablespoons salad oil | 45 | mL |
| 1 | garlic clove, minced | 1 | |
| 1 | pound medium shrimp, raw, shelled and deveined | 500 | g |
| 3 | scallions, cut on the bias | 3 | |
| 1½ | cups snow peas, ends and strings removed | 375 | mL |
| 1 | can (10 oz/284 mL) water chestnuts, drained and thinly sliced | 1 | |

Mix cornstarch, ginger, soy sauce, sherry and broth; set aside. Heat wok over high heat. Add oil. When oil is hot, add garlic and shrimp and stir-fry one minute. Add scallions and snow peas and stir-fry about two minutes. Add water chestnuts and stir to mix. Add cornstarch mixture and stir until it boils and thickens, about one minute. Add more soy sauce, if desired.

**NOTE:** If you are shelling fresh shrimp, leave the tails on for a decorative touch.

**Serves 4**

# Scallops & Mushrooms in Wine

*Elegant and attractive to serve for luncheon or dinner.*

| | | | |
|---|---|---:|---|
| 1½ | cups dry white wine | 375 | mL |
| ½ | cup water | 125 | mL |
| | Bay leaf | | |
| | Sprig of parsley | | |
| | Pinch of thyme | | |
| 2 | pounds of scallops, rinsed and drained | 1 | kg |
| 5 | tablespoons butter, divided | 75 | mL |
| 2 | tablespoons onions, finely chopped | 30 | mL |
| ¾ | pound fresh mushrooms, sliced | 375 | g |
| 1 | tablespoon lemon juice | 15 | mL |
| 2 | teaspoons parsley, chopped | 10 | mL |
| ½ | teaspoon salt | 2 | mL |
| ¼ | teaspoon each white pepper, | 1 | mL |
| | Nutmeg and thyme | | |
| 4 | tablespoons flour | 60 | mL |
| | Pinch of cayenne | | |
| 2 | cups liquid, cooking liquid from scallops | 500 | mL |
| | plus enough 18% cream to make 2 cups | | |
| 6 | tablespoons Parmesan cheese, grated | 90 | mL |
| ½ | cup bread crumbs | 125 | mL |

Preheat oven to 350°F (180°C). In a large saucepan, bring wine, water, bay leaf, sprig of parsley and thyme to a boil. Add scallops and cook gently for 5-6 minutes. Remove scallops, strain broth and reserve. Melt 1 tablespoon (15 mL) butter in a skillet and sauté onions until soft. Add mushrooms and cook until liquid evaporates. Add lemon juice, parsley, salt, pepper, nutmeg and thyme. Stir well and set aside. Melt remaining 4 tablespoons (60 mL) of butter, blend in flour and cook roux 2-3 minutes without browning. Stir in liquid from scallops mixed with cream and cayenne pepper. Cook until thick and smooth. Add 4 tablespoons (60 mL) Parmesan cheese; mix well. Gently fold in scallops, mushrooms and onions and put into a 1-quart (1-L) casserole. Sprinkle with remaining cheese and bread crumbs. Bake until hot and bubbly. The scallops may also be served on individual scallop shells, placed on a baking sheet and baked.
**Serves 6-8**

# Scallops Jambalaya

*All you need is a bottle of chilled wine!*

| | | | |
|---|---|---|---|
| 6 | slices bacon, diced | 6 | |
| 1 | onion, minced | 1 | |
| ½ | cup celery, sliced | 125 | mL |
| 1 | garlic clove, minced | 1 | |
| ½ | teaspoon thyme | 2 | mL |
| | Salt and Tabasco to taste | | |
| 1 | can (28 oz/796 mL) tomatoes, drained | 1 | |
| 2 | cups peas, fresh or frozen | 500 | mL |
| 2 | cups cooked rice | 500 | mL |
| 2 | pounds scallops | 1 | kg |

Cook bacon, onion, celery and garlic over low heat until onion and celery are tender crisp. Do not brown. Add thyme, salt, Tabasco, tomatoes, rice, peas and scallops. Stir gently, cover and simmer slowly for 15 minutes. Do not overcook or scallops will become tough. Serve immediately.

**Serves 6**

# Fruits de Mer Maritime

*A wonderful chafing-dish meal. Can be served as a main course or in seafood shells as an appetizer.*

| | | |
|---|---|---|
| 1 | cup boiling water | 250 mL |
| | Salt | |
| 1 | cup scallops | 250 mL |
| 1 | cup halibut or 2 cups (500 mL) oysters | 250 mL |
| 1 | cup shrimp | 250 mL |
| 1 | cup lobster or crab | 250 mL |
| 1-1½ | cups milk | 250-375 mL |
| 6 | tablespoons butter | 90 mL |
| 6 | tablespoons flour | 90 mL |
| 1 | cup mushrooms, sliced | 250 mL |
| 3 | tablespoons green pepper, diced | 45 mL |
| 3 | tablespoons pimentos, diced | 45 mL |
| ½ | onion, finely chopped | ½ |
| | Dash of Worcestershire sauce | |
| ¼ | teaspoon Dijon mustard | 1 mL |
| ¼ | cup dry white wine | 50 mL |
| 1 | cup 10% cream | 250 mL |

Scald scallops in boiling, salted water for 5 minutes. Drain and reserve liquid. Repeat for halibut or oysters, using just enough liquid to cover. Drain and save liquid. Repeat for shrimp and lobster. Frozen cooked shrimp and lobster will need only heating. To prepare sauce, add enough milk to the reserved fish liquid to make 2 cups (500 mL). Melt butter in a saucepan and stir in flour. Add milk and fish liquid gradually. Stirring constantly and using low heat only, cook until sauce is medium thick. Mixture should not boil! Add mushrooms, green pepper, pimentos, onion, Worcestershire sauce, mustard and wine. Add cream and stir in. Add fish mixture and simmer slowly. Serve over long-grain rice which has been tossed liberally with chives, green onions and parsley.

**Serves 10**

# Christmas Eve Shrimp Curry

*An original Trinidad recipe.*

| | | | |
|---|---|---|---|
| 1-2 | pounds jumbo shrimp, shelled and deveined | 0.5-1 | kg |
| ⅓ | cup butter | 75 | mL |
| 1-2 | garlic cloves, pressed | 1-2 | |
| 1 | cup celery, sliced on bias | 250 | mL |
| 1 | onion, coarsely chopped | 1 | |
| 2-3 | large carrots, julienne stripped | 2-3 | |
| 2 | cups fresh pineapple cubes (or 1 can [19 oz/540 mL] pineapple chunks and juice) | 500 | mL |
| 2-3 | teaspoons curry powder (depending on how hot you like your curry) | 10-15 | mL |
| 1 | tablespoon fresh ginger, grated (or 1½ teaspoons/7 mL ground ginger) | 15 | mL |
| ¼ | cup flour | 50 | mL |
| 2 | cups chicken broth | 500 | mL |
| 1 | lemon, juice and grated rind | 1 | |
| 1 | cup 10% cream or 2% evaporated milk | 250 | mL |
| ½ | teaspoon salt | 2 | mL |

Sauté shrimp in butter and garlic until pink and tender (low heat). Remove shrimp and add celery, onion and carrots. Cook until onion is transparent and carrots crisp. Add pineapple. Simmer 3 minutes. Remove vegetables and pineapple. Add curry, ginger and flour and brown. Add broth, pineapple juice, lemon juice and rind. Cook slowly until smooth and add cream or evaporated milk. Add salt, shrimp and vegetables. Serve hot with buttered rice tossed with fresh chopped chives and parsley. Use side garnishes of shredded coconut, bacon bits, peanuts, sliced bananas and chutney.

**Serves 8**

# Poulet Dijonnais

*A truly elegant dish!*

| | | |
|---|---|---|
| ½ | cup unsalted butter | 125 mL |
| 3 | whole, large chicken breasts, skinned, boned and cut in 1-inch (2.5-cm) strips | 3 |
| | Salt and pepper to taste | |
| ½ | cup sharp Dijon mustard | 125 mL |
| 2 | cups whipping cream | 500 mL |
| 5 | phyllo pastry sheets | 5 |
| ¼ | cup fresh toasted bread crumbs | 50 mL |
| 1 | egg | 1 |
| 1 | tablespoon water | 15 mL |

Melt ¼ cup (50 mL) butter in a large skillet over medium heat. Sprinkle chicken with salt and pepper. Sauté for about 5 minutes. Transfer to a plate and keep warm. Add mustard to skillet. Whisk in cream and blend. Simmer until sauce is well thickened and is reduced by ¼. Strain sauce over chicken, tossing to coat completely. Cool.

Preheat oven to 400°F (200°C). Melt remaining butter. Lay 1 sheet of phyllo pastry on a dry tea towel. While you are working, keep remaining phyllo covered with a damp tea towel as it dries out very quickly. Brush the sheet of phyllo with melted butter. Sprinkle with 1 tablespoon (15 mL) of bread crumbs. Repeat 3 more times. Top with last sheet of phyllo, brushing only the border with butter. Arrange chicken over bottom third of long side of dough, leaving a 2-inch (5-cm) border on all sides. Turn up bottom edge, then fold in sides, partially enclosing chicken. Roll up, jelly roll fashion. Carefully place seam side down on an ungreased cookie sheet with sides. Beat egg with water and use to glaze dough. Bake until phyllo is golden and crisp, about 20-25 minutes. Cut into 2-inch (5-cm) slices and serve immediately.

Chicken in mustard cream is also good as a filling in puff pastry patty cases (vol-au-vents). The chicken in the sauce can be cooked a day in advance. If used as a patty case filling, add 1 red pepper, cut into strips, and 1 cup of thinly sliced mushrooms while cooking the chicken.

**Serves 6**

# Chicken in Cream

*Rich and wonderful!*

| 8   | pieces of chicken, breasts or legs | 8   |      |
|-----|-------------------------------------|-----|------|
| ¼   | cup butter                          | 50  | mL   |
| 2   | medium onions, chopped              | 2   |      |
| 1   | sprig of thyme                      | 1   |      |
|     | Salt to taste                       |     |      |
| 2   | tablespoons flour                   | 30  | mL   |
| ¼   | cup water                           | 50  | mL   |
| 2   | cups whipping cream                 | 500 | mL   |
| ¼   | cup dry white wine                  | 50  | mL   |
|     | Pepper to taste                     |     |      |

Place chicken in a sauté pan with butter, onions and thyme. Season with salt, cover the pan and place it over moderate heat. Check often and adjust the heat so that the meat gives up its moisture but does not brown. When pieces are firm, remove the thyme and onions. Sprinkle the chicken with flour and stir frequently. After 10 minutes, stir in water, scraping any residue from the bottom and sides of pan. Pour about 6 tablespoons (90 mL) of the cream and all of the wine over the chicken. Simmer gently and add remaining cream a little at a time. The sauce should be rich, smooth and of a consistency that will coat a spoon. Simmer for 25-30 minutes. Add pepper, remove pan from heat and let stand 1 minute before serving.

**Serves 4**

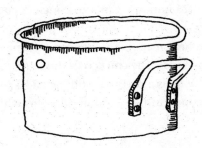

# Curried Chicken Our Way!

*A wonderful main course at a large buffet.*

| | | |
|---|---|---|
| 20 | dried apricots | 20 |
| 2 | cups water | 500 mL |
| 1 | cup raisins | 250 mL |
| 1 | can (10 oz/284 mL) chicken broth or homemade stock | 1 |
| ½ | cup dry white wine | 125 mL |
| | Juice from all fruits, including apricots | |
| 1 | can (14 oz/398 mL) unsweetened pineapple | 1 |
| 1 | can (10 oz/284 mL) mandarin oranges | 1 |
| ½ | cup butter, divided | 125 mL |
| 5 | tablespoons flour | 75 mL |
| 3 | tablespoons powdered chicken stock | 45 mL |
| 2-4 | teaspoons curry powder | 10-20 mL |
| | Salt and pepper to taste | |
| 2½ | pounds chicken breasts, skinned and boned | 1.5 kg |
| 1 | cup seedless green grapes | 250 mL |
| 2 | medium avocados | 2 |
| 1 | cup wide flake coconut | 250 mL |

Simmer apricots in water until tender, about ½ hour. Add raisins the last 5 minutes of cooking time to plump. Combine juices from all fruits, including apricots, with chicken broth and wine; set aside. In food processor or blender, purée 8 apricots, 1 cup (250 mL) pineapple, ¼ cup (50 mL) mandarins and ¼ cup (50 mL) raisins.

Melt 5 tablespoons (75 mL) butter in a large heavy sauce pan. Stir in flour and cook gently for 3-4 minutes. Combine the reserved liquids, fruit purée and powdered chicken stock; add to butter mixture, whisking quickly. Cook until smooth and thick. Add curry and season with salt and pepper. Meanwhile, cut chicken into walnut-sized pieces and sauté in remaining butter just until cooked. Fold chicken, grapes, remaining apricots, pineapple, raisins and mandarins into thickened purée. At this point, curry may be refrigerated or frozen. Reheat gently just before serving and transfer into a large, shallow serving dish or casserole. Garnish with avocados and coconut.
**Serves 16**

# Capon with Cider and Cream

*Succulent is the only word to describe it!*

| | | | |
|---|---|---|---|
| 1 | 5-6 pound (2-3 kg) capon | 1 | |
| 4 | pounds tart cooking apples, such as Spy | 2 | kg |
| 2 | tablespoons lemon juice | 30 | mL |
| ½ | cup butter, divided | 125 | mL |
| 2 | tablespoons oil | 30 | mL |
| 1 | teaspoon ginger, divided | 5 | mL |
| ¼-½ | cup brandy | 50-125 | mL |
| 4-5 | shallots, minced | 4-5 | |
| | Dash of thyme | | |
| 2 | cloves | 2 | |
| 2 | teaspoons sugar | 10 | mL |
| 2 | cups cider | 500 | mL |
| 1 | teaspoon cornstarch | 5 | mL |
| 1 | cup cream, your choice | 250 | mL |
| | Salt and pepper to taste | | |
| 1 | teaspoon parsley or chervil, minced | 5 | mL |

Preheat oven to 400°F (200°C). Peel, core and quarter apples; sprinkle with lemon juice. In a large heavy skillet, heat ⅓ cup (75 mL) butter and the oil. Add half the apples and sauté for 5 minutes. Remove and season lightly with ginger. Sprinkle inside of capon with salt and pepper and fill with sautéed apples. Save the cooking juices. Put capon in a large heavy pot and set, uncovered, in the oven for 20 minutes, turning often to brown all over. Remove from oven and set over moderate heat on top of stove. Warm brandy and pour over top. Ignite. Add 2 tablespoons (30 mL) butter and stir in the shallots, the remaining apples, additional ginger, thyme, cloves and sugar. Cook gently for 5-6 minutes. Add the reserved juices from the apples and the cider and bring to a simmer. Butter a piece of waxed paper generously and cover the capon with it. Now, cover the pan with a lid and return to the oven for 1-2 hours until capon is cooked.

**TO SERVE:** Remove the capon to a warm platter. Strain the cooking juices and remove the fat. Return to a pan and reduce over high heat to about 1½ cups (250-375 mL). Dissolve cornstarch in a little cream, then blend in the rest of the cream and pour it into the juices. Stir as it thickens. Carve the capon and arrange on a platter with the apple stuffing in the middle. Pour over a little sauce, sprinkle with parsley or chervil and serve. Pass sauce separately.
**Serves 6**

## Ginger and Lemon Chicken

*Delicious family dinner. Good on the barbecue, too!*

| | | |
|---|---|---|
| ¼ | **cup butter or olive or hazelnut oil** | 50 mL |
| 2 | **teaspoons lemon peel, grated** | 10 mL |
| 2 | **tablespoons lemon juice** | 30 mL |
| ½ | **teaspoon salt** | 2 mL |
| ¼ | **teaspoon paprika** | 1 mL |
| 1 | **tablespoon freshly grated ginger** | 15 mL |
| | **Dash of Tabasco sauce** | |
| 4 | **chicken breasts (2 whole split)** | 4 |

Heat butter or oil on low; stir in the next 6 ingredients. Place chicken, skin side down, on a rack. Broil on lowest rack for about 15-20 minutes, basting with sauce. Turn breasts over and continue broiling and basting for a further 15-20 minutes.
**Serves 4**

# Amaretto Chicken

*Unique and so easy!*

| | | |
|---|---|---|
| 5 | whole boned chicken breasts, halved | 5 |
| 3 | tablespoons flour | 45 mL |
| 1 | teaspoon salt | 5 mL |
| 1½ | teaspoons ground pepper | 7 mL |
| 2 | teaspoons paprika | 10 mL |
| 1 | garlic clove, minced | 1 |
| 1 | tablespoon vegetable oil | 15 mL |
| 3 | tablespoons butter | 45 mL |
| 1½ | tablespoons Dijon mustard | 25 mL |
| 1 | can (6¼ oz/178 mL) frozen orange juice, thawed and mixed with ½ can water | 1 |
| ½-1 | cup Amaretto | 125-250 mL |

Preheat oven to 350°F (180°C). Combine flour, salt, pepper and paprika. Coat chicken with this mixture. Heat oil and butter in skillet and sauté garlic and chicken until brown. Remove and put in casserole. To skillet, add mustard, orange juice and Amaretto. Increase heat and boil, stirring constantly, until thick. Pour sauce over chicken and bake, covered, for 45 minutes. If desired, freeze and reheat later.

**Serves 8-10**

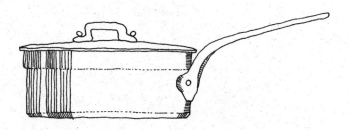

# Cool Curry Chicken

*A delicious curry that can be served hot or cold.*

| 6-8 | half breasts of chicken, skinned and boned | 6-8 | |
|-----|---------------------------------------------|-----|-----|
| ¼ | cup butter | 50 | mL |
| ½ | cup honey | 125 | mL |
| ¼ | cup Dijon mustard | 50 | mL |
| 2 | tablespoons prepared mustard | 30 | mL |
| 1 | tablespoon curry powder | 15 | mL |
| ½ | lime, juice and rind finely grated | ½ | |
| 1 | teaspoon salt | 5 | mL |
| 1 | garlic clove, minced | 1 | |

Preheat oven to 350°F (180°C). Arrange chicken in a single layer in a Pyrex baking dish. In a metal saucepan, combine remaining ingredients and bring to a boil. Remove from heat and pour over chicken. Bake for 45 minutes. Baste from time to time if necessary. Can be served hot over rice or cold for a summer buffet with rice salad.
**Serves 6-8**

# Chicken with Nectarines

*Excellent, easy and fast! Try adding a bit of dry sherry or a pinch of curry powder to the sauce.*

| | | |
|---|---|---|
| 6 | half chicken breasts, boned | 6 |
| 4 | tablespoons butter | 60 mL |
| 4 | nectarines, peeled, pitted and quartered* | 4 |
| ½-1 | cup whipping cream | 125-250 mL |
| | Salt and pepper to taste | |

Place chicken breasts, one at a time, between 2 sheets of waxed paper and gently pound with rolling pin until flattened and about ¼ inch (0.5 cm) thick. Sauté in butter on one side for 5 minutes. Turn, add nectarines and continue to sauté for another 5-10 minutes until done. Remove chicken and nectarines to heated platter and keep warm in oven.

**SAUCE:** Add cream slowly to pan drippings and mix thoroughly with wire whisk. Continue to whisk over medium heat until sauce thickens. Season to taste. Pour over chicken and nectarines. Serve immediately.
**Serves 4-6**

**\*TIP:** Try peaches or seedless green grapes instead of nectarines.

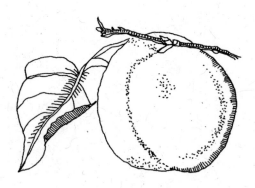

# Chicken Breast with Avocado

*This elegant entrée has a delicate flavour which should not compete with side dishes.*

| | | | |
|---|---|---|---|
| 2 | pounds chicken breasts, boned and skinned | 1 | kg |
| ½ | pound large mushrooms | 250 | g |
| 4 | tablespoons butter | 60 | mL |
| | Salt and freshly ground pepper | | |
| | Pinch of nutmeg | | |
| ¼ | cup shallots, finely chopped | 50 | mL |
| 2 | leeks, whites only, finely chopped | 2 | |
| ¼ | cup cognac | 50 | mL |
| 2 | cups whipping cream | 500 | mL |
| 1 | large avocado | 1 | |
| | Pinch of cayenne | | |

Trim chicken, removing all sinews. Cut into 1-inch (2.5-cm) pieces. Trim stems off mushrooms and cut caps into ½-inch (1-cm) pieces. Heat butter in large skillet; add chicken. Sprinkle with salt, pepper and nutmeg. Cook over high heat, stirring, about 5 minutes or until tender. Remove chicken to heat-proof serving dish. Add mushrooms, shallots and leeks to skillet, cook 1 minute, add cognac and stir. Add cream and cook down over medium heat, about 8-10 minutes. Add juices that may accumulate around chicken. Cut avocado into 8 pieces, lengthwise. Halve these crosswise. Add cayenne and avocado. Heat through. Pour sauce over chicken, heat through and serve immediately.

**Serves 4-6**

# Fettuccine Verde con Pollo

| | | |
|---|---|---|
| 1 | 5-pound (2.5-kg) chicken | 1 |
| 1 | onion | 1 |
| 1 | carrot | 1 |
| 1 | stalk celery, with leaves | 1 |
| | Salt to taste | |
| | Bouquet garni—10 black peppercorns (barely crushed), 1 garlic clove, pinch of thyme, 1 bay leaf and 6 parsley stems, all tied in cheesecloth | |
| ½ | cup butter or fat from the chicken | 125 mL |
| ⅔ | cup flour | 150 mL |
| 3 | cups reserved chicken stock | 750 mL |
| 1 | can (10 oz/284 mL) mushrooms with liquid | 1 |
| ¾ | teaspoon garlic powder | 4 mL |
| 1 | teaspoon salt | 5 mL |
| 3 | tablespoons dry white wine | 45 mL |
| 5 | cups Parmesan cheese, grated—yes, 5 cups! | 1.25 L |
| 10 | ounces spinach noodles | 284 g |
| 3 | cups bread, broken into small pieces | 750 mL |
| 4 | tablespoons butter | 60 mL |
| 4 | ounces slivered almonds | 125 g |

Place chicken into a large pot; add cold water to cover by about 2 inches (5 cm). Bring to a slow boil, uncovered, over moderate heat. Skim any scum off the surface. Add the onion, carrot, celery, salt and bouquet garni. Lower the heat and simmer gently, cover ajar, for 1½ to 2 hours. Remove chicken and cool. Separate the chicken from the bones and cut into large pieces. Skim the fat from the stock. This is much easier if it has been refrigerated overnight.

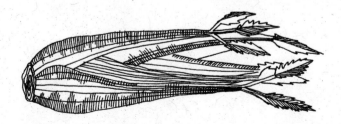

Meanwhile, in a large saucepan, melt the butter. Add the flour, stir well and cook for 1 minute. Add the stock, mushrooms, garlic and salt; mix. Add wine and Parmesan cheese. Cook, stirring constantly, until thick. Mixture should be very thick. Cook noodles until barely tender. Do not overcook! Drain and rinse well in cold water. Butter a 9" × 13" (3.5 L) glass dish. To assemble, layer the noodles, chicken and sauce in the baking dish. Repeat so that there are 2 layers of each. The dish can be frozen at this point. When ready to serve, pre-heat oven to 350°F (180°C). Sauté bread chunks in butter. Bake chicken for 30-45 minutes. About 5 minutes before chicken is ready, spread crumbs and almonds on top of casserole and return to oven to brown.

**Serves 12-16**

# Veal with Mushrooms and Wine

| | | | |
|---|---|---|---|
| 1½ | pounds veal scallopini | 750 | g |
| 2 | tablespoons flour | 30 | mL |
| 2 | tablespoons butter | 30 | mL |
| ½ | pound mushrooms, thinly sliced | 250 | g |
| 1 | tablespoon onion, finely chopped | 15 | mL |
| ½ | cup dry white wine | 125 | mL |
| 1 | cup whipping cream | 250 | mL |
| 1 | tablespoon lemon juice | 15 | mL |
| | Salt, pepper and garlic powder to taste | | |

Cut veal into pieces and flour very lightly. Fry quickly in butter. Remove from pan and keep in a warm oven. Sauté onions and mushrooms in the same pan. Add wine and cream and reduce over medium heat until thick. Stir in lemon juice, salt, pepper and garlic. Pour over scallopini and serve with noodles or rice. Best served immediately.

**Serves 4**

# Veal and Water Chestnuts

*Use the shoulder for an economical party meal.*

| | | | |
|---|---|---|---|
| 2 | pounds boneless veal cut in 1" (2.5 cm) cubes | 1 | kg |
| 2 | tablespoons olive oil | 30 | mL |
| 1 | medium onion, chopped | 1 | |
| 1 | garlic clove, minced | 1 | |
| 1 | teaspoon salt | 5 | mL |
| ¼ | teaspoon pepper | 1 | mL |
| | Dash of cayenne | | |
| 1 | pound mushrooms, quartered | 500 | g |
| 1 | cup beef bouillon | 250 | mL |
| 1 | can (10 oz/284 mL) water chestnuts, sliced | 1 | |
| | Dash of nutmeg | | |
| 1 | bay leaf | 1 | |
| 1 | cup whipping cream | 250 | mL |
| ¼ | cup cognac | 50 | mL |
| ¼ | cup parsley, chopped | 50 | mL |

Preheat oven to 350°F (180°C). Brown veal in oil in a large skillet.
Stir in onion and garlic; cook until onion is golden. Season with
salt, pepper and cayenne. Transfer veal and onions to a 2-quart (2-L)
casserole with a slotted spoon. In the same skillet, sauté mushrooms,
adding a little more oil if necessary. Add to casserole along with
bouillon, water chestnuts, nutmeg and bay leaf. Cover and bake 1½
hours until meat is tender. Stir in cream and cook 15 minutes longer,
uncovered. Add cognac and parsley.
**Serves 6-8**

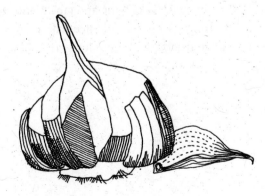

# Pork Tenderloin with Orange Sauce

*Cook the pork ahead of time and put the sauce together at serving time.*

| | | | |
|---|---|---|---|
| ¼ | cup flour | 50 | mL |
| 1 | teaspoon salt | 5 | mL |
| ½ | teaspoon paprika | 2 | mL |
| ¼ | teaspoon pepper | 1 | mL |
| ¼ | teaspoon allspice | 1 | mL |
| 1 | pound pork tenderloin, sliced into 12 rounds and slightly flattened | 500 | g |
| 2 | tablespoons cooking oil | 30 | mL |
| ¼ | cup chicken stock | 50 | mL |
| ½ | cup sour cream | 125 | mL |
| 2 | tablespoons orange juice | 30 | mL |
| 1 | tablespoon orange rind, grated | 15 | mL |
| ¼ | teaspoon salt | 1 | mL |
| ½ | teaspoon Worcestershire sauce | 2 | mL |
| 1 | tablespoon orange liqueur | 15 | mL |

Combine flour, salt, pepper, paprika and allspice. Coat rounds of
tenderloin. Heat oil in a heavy skillet and brown pork well. Add stock,
cover and simmer for 30 minutes. Combine remaining ingredients
in a small pan. Heat but do not boil. Serve drained pork over white
or, better yet, wild rice. Pour sauce over all and serve. Garnish with
parsley and orange slices.

**Serves 4**

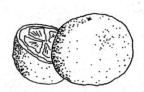

# Roast Pork Cointreau

*Absolutely the best pork roast we've ever tasted!*

| | | | |
|---|---|---|---|
| 4-6 | pounds boneless pork loin roast | 2-3 | kg |
| ½ | teaspoon thyme | 2 | mL |
| ¼ | teaspoon pepper | 1 | mL |
| 2 | garlic cloves, finely minced | 2 | |
| 2 | oranges, rind and juice | 2 | |
| 1 | tablespoon oil | 15 | mL |
| 1 | onion, chopped | 1 | |
| 1 | carrot, chopped | 1 | |
| 1 | stalk celery, chopped | 1 | |
| 1 | bouquet garni of 2 sprigs parsley, 1 bay leaf and thyme | 1 | |
| ½ | cup Cointreau or Triple Sec | 125 | mL |
| 2 | tablespoons brown sugar | 30 | mL |
| 2 | tablespoons wine vinegar | 30 | mL |
| 2 | tablespoons butter, softened | 30 | mL |
| 2 | tablespoons flour | 30 | mL |

Mix thyme, pepper and garlic together; rub over roast. Allow to marinate 4 hours or overnight in the refrigerator. Remove rind from the oranges and cut into julienne strips. Blanch in boiling water for 2 minutes. Drain and pat dry on paper towels and set aside. Juice the 2 oranges and set aside.

Preheat oven to 350°F (180°C). Dry roast and scrape off most of the seasonings. Reserve any juices. Brown meat on all sides in 1 tablespoon (15 mL) oil in an enamelled pan. Remove the roast, reserve the juices and leave 1 tablespoon (15 mL) of fat in the pan. Sauté the onion, carrot and celery until tender and transparent. Return the roast to the pan and add the bouquet garni. Roast, covered with foil, for 45 minutes. Reserve and strain juices. Transfer meat to a roasting pan and roast, uncovered, 1¼ hours or until the juices run clear when meat is pricked with a fork. Remove to a serving platter and keep warm.

Skim fat from pan. Add ¼ cup (50 mL) Cointreau and flame, scraping all the browned bits. Shake the pan until the flame goes out. Simmer for 5 minutes. Add sugar and wine vinegar and reduce to a light caramel colour. Add strained pan juices and orange juice. Combine flour and butter and add bit by bit, stirring, to make a smooth, thick gravy. Arrange orange rind over the roast. Warm the remaining Cointreau and flame over roast. Serve immediately with sauce.
**Serves 8-10**

# Marinated Pork Loin Roast

*Wait until you smell this cooking!*

| | | | |
|---|---|---|---|
| 4-5 | pound pork loin roast, boned and rolled | 2 | kg |
| ½ | cup soy sauce | 125 | mL |
| ½ | cup sherry | 125 | mL |
| 2 | garlic cloves, minced | 2 | |
| 1 | tablespoon dry mustard | 15 | mL |
| 1 | tablespoon freshly grated ginger (or | 15 | mL |
| | 1 teaspoon/5 mL ginger powder) | | |
| 1 | teaspoon thyme, crushed | 5 | mL |

**SAUCE**

| | | | |
|---|---|---|---|
| 1 | 10-ounce (284-mL) jar black currant jelly | 1 | |
| 1 | tablespoon soy sauce | 15 | mL |
| 2 | tablespoons sherry | 30 | mL |

Place meat in plastic bag. Mix soy sauce, sherry, garlic, mustard, ginger and thyme and pour over meat. Marinate for 5 hours or overnight. Remove from plastic bag and place meat in a roasting pan. Preheat oven to 325°F (160°C). Roast, uncovered, for 2½ to 3 hours, basting frequently.

To make sauce, combine all the ingredients and heat for about 2 minutes. Serve with meat.
**Serves 10**

# Beef Magnifique

*A good hearty bourguignon!*

| | | | |
|---|---|---|---|
| ½ | pound salt pork, thinly sliced, or bacon | 250 | g |
| 2 | dozen small white onions | 24 | |
| 4 | pounds lean beef, cut in small cubes | 2 | kg |
| 1 | teaspoon flour | 5 | mL |
| ½ | teaspoon salt | 2 | mL |
| ½ | teaspoon freshly ground pepper | 2 | mL |
| 1 | garlic clove, minced | 1 | |
| 1 | slice orange peel | 1 | |
| 2 | cans (each 10 oz/284 mL) beef consommé | 2 | |
| 2 | cups dry red wine (Burgundy) | 500 | mL |
| 1 | cup fresh small button mushrooms | 250 | mL |
| | Fresh parsley, finely chopped | | |
| 1 | bouquet garni (which contains 2 small bay leaves, 1 sprig thyme, ¼ teaspoon [1 mL] freshly ground nutmeg, 1 sprig marjoram and small bunch of parsley—if fresh spices are not available, a teaspoon [5 mL] of dried will do) | 1 | |

Preheat oven to 300°F (150°C). Brown salt pork or bacon in Dutch oven until crisp. Remove pork and brown onions in remaining fat. Remove onions. Brown meat on all sides in same fat. Sprinkle pork with flour; return to Dutch oven. Season with salt and pepper. Add garlic, orange peel, bouquet garni, wine and consommé. Cover tightly and place in oven for about 3 hours. Add more wine as necessary. Sauté fresh mushrooms in a little butter. Add mushrooms and onions for another 30 minutes cooking time. Remove from oven; discard the bouquet garni and orange peel. Sprinkle lavishly with fresh parsley.

**Serves 8-10**

# Stuffed Flank Steak Roll

| | | |
|---|---|---|
| 2 | flank steaks | 2 |
| | Salt and pepper to taste | |
| ½ | cup onions, chopped | 125 mL |
| 3 | tablespoons butter or oil | 45 mL |
| ½ | pound mushrooms, chopped | 250 g |
| ½ | pound bulk sausage meat | 250 g |
| ¾ | cup fine, dry bread crumbs | 175 mL |
| ½ | teaspoon salt | 2 mL |
| | Pinch of thyme and pepper | |
| 2 | tablespoons olive oil | 30 mL |
| 1 | beef bouillon cube | 1 |
| 1 | cup water | 250 mL |

Preheat oven to 325°F (160°C). Trim fat and connective tissue from steaks. Score on both sides to tenderize and sprinkle with salt and pepper. Pan-fry onions in butter until almost tender. Stir in mushrooms and cook 3-4 minutes longer. Add the next 5 ingredients; stir and cook until sausage loses most of its pinkness. Drain and spread over one steak, cover with the second. Tie to form a cylinder with the stuffing in the centre. Brown steak on top of stove in a roasting pan in the oil. Dissolve beef bouillon in water and pour over steak. Cook uncovered in oven until tender, 2-2½ hours. Remove to a warm platter and make gravy using pan drippings.
**Serves 4-6**

# Flank Steak Teriyaki

*A barbecue sensation!*

| | | | |
|---|---|---|---|
| ¼ | cup oil | 50 | mL |
| ¼ | cup soy sauce | 50 | mL |
| ¼ | cup honey | 50 | mL |
| 1 | large garlic clove, minced | 1 | |
| 2 | tablespoons vinegar | 30 | mL |
| 1 | onion, grated | 1 | |
| 2 | tablespoons fresh ginger, grated | 30 | mL |
| 1 | flank steak | 1 | |

Mix all marinade ingredients together and pour over flank steak in a glass or enamel bowl. Marinate a minimum of 4 hours or overnight. Barbecue (or broil in oven) 5 minutes each side for rare. Carve in very thin strips across grain of meat and serve at once.

**Serves 4**

# Beef Wellington

*This is an easy but impressive dish which can be prepared in the morning and baked just before serving. Guaranteed to be medium rare!*

| | | |
|---|---|---|
| 1 | 3-4 pound (1.5-2 kg) filet of beef | 1 |
| | Salt and pepper | |
| 1 | pound mushrooms, finely chopped | 500 g |
| 3 | scallions, finely chopped | 3 |
| 1 | tablespoon butter | 15 mL |
| 2 | tablespoons flour | 30 mL |
| 1 | teaspoon lemon juice | 5 mL |
| 1 | tablespoon sherry | 15 mL |
| 1 | can (3 oz/90 g) liver pâté | 1 |
| 1 | package (14 oz/397 g) frozen puff pastry | 1 |
| 1 | egg, separated | 1 |

Preheat oven to 425°F (220°C). Bring filet to room temperature and roast for 20 minutes. Season with salt and pepper; cool thoroughly. Simmer mushrooms and scallions in butter for 15 minutes. Stir in flour, lemon juice, sherry and pâté. Cook for a few minutes and cool. Mixture should be thick. If there are any excess juices, drain. Roll out pastry on floured surface. Do not roll too thin or juices will leak out while baking. Grease and flour a cookie sheet or large baking pan. Set pastry in pan to assemble. This will save lifting later. Place beef in centre of pastry. Spread mushroom/pâté mixture on the top and partially down sides. Neatly fold up sides and edges, sealing with egg white. With remaining pastry, make a long braid and place over sealed edge. Decorate with pastry if desired. Combine the remaining egg white with egg yolk and brush the surface. Beef Wellington can be refrigerated at this stage and baked later. Return to room temperature and bake for 35 minutes. Let stand for 10 minutes before carving. Meat will be medium rare every time!

**Serves 6-8**

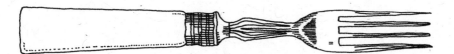

# Marinated Boned Leg of Lamb

*An elegant entrée for a summer barbecue!*

| 1 | leg of lamb | 1 | |
|---|---|---|---|

## MARINADE

| ½ | cup olive oil | 125 | mL |
|---|---|---|---|
| ⅔ | cup lemon juice | 150 | mL |
| 3 | large garlic cloves, minced | 3 | |
| 2 | bay leaves | 2 | |
| 6 | sprigs parsley | 6 | |
| 2 | teaspoons salt | 10 | mL |
| 1½ | teaspoons sage or ground cloves | 7 | mL |
| 1½ | teaspoons each rosemary and thyme | 7 | mL |

## SAUCE

| ½ | cup beef stock | 125 | mL |
|---|---|---|---|
| ½ | cup red wine | 125 | mL |
| 2 | tablespoons marinade | 30 | mL |
| 1 | teaspoon sage or cloves | 5 | mL |
| 1 | teaspoon each rosemary and thyme | 5 | mL |
| 3 | tablespoons soft butter | 45 | mL |
| 3 | tablespoons parsley, chopped | 45 | mL |

Bone and skin a leg of lamb. (It is easier to do when the meat is partially frozen. Easier still, get a good butcher to do it!) Combine the marinade ingredients in a glass or enamel pan and marinate the lamb for 24 hours, turning occasionally. Drain, and sear lamb on both sides over very hot coals. Lower heat and cook until pink, about 45 minutes to 1 hour.

For the sauce, combine all the ingredients except the butter and parsley and boil rapidly to reduce to ½ cup (125 mL). Remove from heat; add butter and parsley. Pour a bit over meat and pass the rest at the table. Slice roast across the grain.

Serves 6-8

# Vegetables and Other Accompaniments

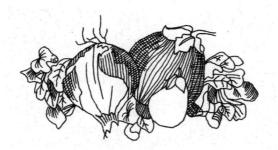

# Italian Style Vegetables

*Great at harvest time—delicious all year round!*

| | | |
|---|---|---|
| 3-4 | medium zucchini, sliced | 3-4 |
| 1 | large Spanish onion, sliced into rings | 1 |
| 1 | medium green pepper, sliced into strips | 1 |
| 1 | medium red pepper, sliced into strips | 1 |
| 3-4 | medium potatoes, sliced | 3-4 |
| 1 | teaspoon basil | 5 mL |
| 1 | teaspoon oregano | 5 mL |
| | Garlic powder, salt and pepper to taste | |
| ½ | cup Romano or Parmesan cheese, grated | 125 mL |
| ½ | cup bread crumbs | 125 mL |
| ½ | cup oil | 125 mL |

Preheat oven to 350°F (180°C). Layer vegetables in a greased casserole. Sprinkle each layer with seasonings. Mix cheese and crumbs together and sprinkle on top. Drizzle oil over all and bake for 30 minutes.
**Serves 8-10**

# Vegetable Supreme

| | | | |
|---|---|---|---|
| 2 | cups fresh broccoli florets and tender stems | 500 | mL |
| 2 | cups fresh cauliflower florets | 500 | mL |
| 2 | eggs | 2 | |
| ½ | cup mayonnaise, regular or light | 125 | mL |
| 1 | medium onion, finely chopped | 1 | |
| 1 | can (10 oz/284 mL) cream of mushroom soup, undiluted | 1 | |
| 1 | cup sharp Cheddar cheese, grated | 250 | mL |
| ½ | cup butter, melted | 125 | mL |
| 1 | box (6 oz/170 g) seasoned croutons, crushed | 1 | |

Preheat oven to 350°F (180°C). Distribute vegetables evenly in lightly buttered 11" × 7" (3 L) casserole. Beat eggs; combine with mayonnaise, onion, mushroom soup and ½ cup (125 mL) grated cheese. Pour evenly over vegetables. Sprinkle remaining cheese over top and level gently with back of spoon. Pour melted butter over entire top of casserole. Distribute crushed croutons over melted butter—they will absorb butter as casserole bakes. Bake for 40 minutes.
Serves 12

**COMMENTS:** A beautiful dish to serve. Should be prepared early in the day (or even a day ahead) so that the flavours blend and the topping mellows. Bake just before serving.

# Ghivetch

*Excellent served with beef or pork—a harvest-time treat!*

| | | |
|---|---|---|
| 1 | cup carrots, sliced | 250 mL |
| 1 | cup fresh green beans, ½" (1 cm) diagonal slices | 250 mL |
| 1 | cup potatoes, diced | 250 mL |
| ½ | cup celery, ¼" (0.5 cm) diagonal slices | 125 mL |
| 1 | small yellow squash, cubed | 1 |
| 1 | small zucchini, thinly sliced | 1 |
| ½ | Bermuda onion, thinly sliced | ½ |
| ½ | small cauliflower, broken into florets | ½ |
| ¼ | cup sweet red pepper, in julienne strips | 50 mL |
| ¼ | cup green pepper, in julienne strips | 50 mL |
| ½ | cup frozen peas | 125 mL |
| 1 | cup beef bouillon | 250 mL |
| ⅓ | cup olive oil | 75 mL |
| 3 | small garlic cloves, minced | 3 |
| 1 | teaspoon salt | 5 mL |
| ½ | bay leaf, crumbled | ½ |
| ½ | teaspoon savory | 2 mL |
| ¼ | teaspoon tarragon | 1 mL |
| 2 | medium tomatoes, quartered, or 12 cherry tomatoes | 2 |

Preheat oven to 350°F (180°C). Prepare all vegetables and mix together in an ungreased 9" × 13" (3.5 L) shallow baking dish. Put bouillon in a small saucepan. Add the oil, garlic, bay leaf, savory and tarragon; heat until boiling. Pour over vegetables. Cover with a tight lid or foil and bake for 45-50 minutes until vegetables are tender. Do not overcook. Stir occasionally to insure even cooking. Add tomatoes for the last 15 minutes of the cooking time.

**Serves 10-12**

# Winter Vegetable Bake

*Colourful and zingy!*

| | | | |
|---|---|---|---|
| 2 | cups carrots, sliced on the diagonal | 500 | mL |
| 2 | cups brussels sprouts | 500 | mL |
| ½ | cup mayonnaise, regular or light | 125 | mL |
| 2 | tablespoons onion, finely chopped | 30 | mL |
| 2 | tablespoons prepared horseradish | 30 | mL |
| ½ | teaspoon each salt and pepper | 2 | mL |
| ½ | cup fresh bread crumbs | 125 | mL |
| 1 | tablespoon butter | 15 | mL |
| 2 | tablespoons parsley, chopped | 30 | mL |

Preheat oven to 350°F (180°C). Cook carrots and sprouts in boiling salted water for 10 minutes or until crisp tender. Drain, reserving ¼ cup (50 mL) of the liquid. Place vegetables and liquid in a casserole. Mix mayonnaise, onion, horseradish, salt and pepper together and spoon over vegetables. Combine butter, crumbs and parsley and sprinkle on top. Bake uncovered for 20-25 minutes until heated through. **Serves 6**

# Mushroom and Eggplant Moussaka

*Could be a meal in itself!*

| | | | |
|---|---|---|---|
| 3 | medium eggplants, cut into ½-inch (1-cm) slices | 3 | |
| 2 | pounds mushrooms, sliced | 1 | kg |
| 3 | tablespoons butter | 45 | mL |
| 1 | large onion, chopped | 1 | |
| 2 | garlic cloves, minced | 2 | |
| 1 | can (5½ oz/156 mL) tomato paste | 1 | |
| ¼ | cup fresh parsley, chopped | 50 | mL |
| ½ | teaspoon each of oregano and basil | 2 | mL |
| ½ | teaspoon salt | 2 | mL |
| | Freshly ground pepper to taste | | |
| | Dash of cinnamon | | |
| ¼ | cup dry red wine | 50 | mL |
| ½ | cup bread crumbs | 125 | mL |
| ½ | cup Parmesan or Cheddar or Jarlsberg, grated | 125 | mL |
| 4 | eggs, beaten | 4 | |

## WHITE SAUCE

| | | | |
|---|---|---|---|
| ½ | cup butter | 125 | mL |
| ½ | cup flour | 125 | mL |
| 3 | cups warm milk | 750 | mL |
| 4 | egg yolks (optional) | 4 | |

## TOPPING

| | | | |
|---|---|---|---|
| ½ | cup bread crumbs | 125 | mL |
| | Extra Cheddar or Jarlsberg, grated, to sprinkle on top | | |

Preheat oven to 350°F (180°C). Salt eggplants lightly and allow to stand on a tea towel 15 minutes. Bake on oiled cookie sheet for 15 minutes. Remove. Sauté mushrooms in butter with chopped onion and garlic until limp. Add tomato paste, parsley, oregano, basil, salt, pepper, cinnamon and red wine. Simmer until liquid is absorbed. Add bread crumbs, grated cheese and beaten eggs. Remove from heat.

## WHITE SAUCE:

Melt butter in saucepan, add flour and mix well. Cook for 2-3 minutes. Stir in warm milk and whisk constantly until sauce is thick. If using egg yolks, beat and add to white sauce. Remove from heat. Butter a 3-quart (3-L) casserole. Cover bottom with eggplants. Spread half the mushroom sauce on top. Repeat with remaining eggplants and sauce. Top with the white sauce; sprinkle with breadcrumbs and cheese. Bake for 35 minutes covered. Uncover and bake for another 15 minutes.
**Serves 8-10**

# Melitzantomati

*Even eggplant haters like this Greek dish!*

| | | | |
|---|---|---|---|
| 1 | medium eggplant | 1 | |
| 1 | can (14 oz/398 mL) tomato sauce | 1 | |
| 1 | large sweet onion, chopped | 1 | |
| 1 | garlic clove, minced | 1 | |
| 1½ | tablespoons olive oil | 25 | mL |
| 1 | teaspoon basil, crushed | 5 | mL |
| ½ | cup Parmesan cheese, grated | 125 | mL |

Preheat oven to 350°F (180°C). Cut stem from eggplant and cut into 1-inch (2.5-cm) cubes. Place in a buttered 1½- to 2-quart (2-L) deep casserole. Mix tomato sauce, onions, garlic, oil and basil. Pour over eggplant and bake, covered, for 30 minutes. Stir, sprinkle with cheese and bake, uncovered, for 15 to 20 minutes more.
**Serves 6**

# Ratatouille

*A Provençal classic—delicious hot or cold!*

| | | |
|---|---|---|
| 2 | tablespoons olive oil | 30 mL |
| 2 | medium onions, coarsely chopped | 2 |
| 1 | green pepper, chopped | 1 |
| 2 | garlic cloves, minced | 2 |
| ¼ | cup parsley, chopped | 50 mL |
| 1 | can (19 oz/540 mL) Italian tomatoes | 1 |
| | Salt and pepper to taste | |
| 1 | teaspoon oregano | 5 mL |
| ½ | teaspoon basil | 2 mL |
| 1 | bay leaf | 1 |
| 1 | medium eggplant, unpeeled | 1 |
| 1 | medium zucchini | 1 |
| 2 | tablespoons oil (may need more) | 30 mL |

In a large sauce pan, heat oil and add onions, green pepper and garlic. Cook slowly until onions are limp. Add parsley, tomatoes and seasonings. Bring to a boil, lower heat and simmer until blended. Wash eggplant and zucchini; trim ends. Cut eggplant into 1-inch (2.5-cm) cubes and zucchini into ½-inch (1-cm) slices. In a skillet, sauté the two vegetables a few pieces at a time in oil until lightly browned. Sprinkle with salt and pepper as they fry, and drain on paper towels. Add to simmering tomato sauce. Partially cover and cook over low heat about 45 minutes, stirring occasionally.

**Serves 4-6**

# Crisp Zucchini Bake

*Tasty and attractive!*

| | | | |
|---|---|---|---|
| 1 | cup red onion rings | 250 | mL |
| 1 | cup green pepper rings | 250 | mL |
| 2 | tablespoons olive oil | 30 | mL |
| 2 | cups zucchini, sliced 1 inch (2.5 cm) thick | 500 | mL |
| 4 | tomatoes, peeled and cut in wedges | 4 | |
| | or 16 cherry tomatoes, halved | | |
| | Salt and pepper to taste | | |
| | Parmesan cheese | | |

Preheat oven to 350°F (180°C). In a large frying pan, sauté onion and green pepper in oil. When wilted, add zucchini and sauté until tender, about 5 minutes. Add tomatoes and cook until soft. Season with salt and pepper. Turn into a 1-quart (1-L) baking dish and sprinkle with cheese. Bake just until topping browns and vegetables are hot.

**Serves 4-6**

# Spinach Stuffed Onions

*A little out of the ordinary.*

| | | |
|---|---|---|
| 8 | Spanish onions | 8 |
| 3 | bunches fresh spinach, washed and trimmed | 3 |
| ½ | teaspoon salt | 2 mL |
| ¼ | teaspoon pepper | 1 mL |
| ¼ | teaspoon ground nutmeg | 1 mL |
| 1 | tablespoon fresh lemon juice | 15 mL |
| 2 | tablespoons freshly grated Parmesan cheese | 30 mL |
| 2 | tablespoons butter | 30 mL |
| 2 | tablespoons flour | 30 mL |
| ¼ | cup sour cream | 50 mL |
| 2 | eggs, beaten | 2 |

Peel the onions and place them in boiling water to cover, using a
4-quart (4-L) kettle. Reduce the heat to medium and cook the onions
for 15 minutes. Remove the onions from the kettle and drain well in
a colander. Cool and hollow out the centres, leaving approximately
a ⅓-inch (1-cm) thick shell. Reserve the centres of the onion for
another use. In a saucepan with a cover, cook the spinach leaves over
low heat, adding no water except for that clinging to the leaves from
the washing. Cook, covered, for 4-5 minutes or until limp. In a
colander, squeeze all the water from the spinach, and chop it finely.
Place the chopped spinach in a medium-sized mixing bowl and add
the salt, pepper, nutmeg, lemon juice and cheese.

Place the butter in a heavy skillet over low heat. As the butter
melts, slowly add the flour, stirring constantly to make a roux,
about 2-3 minutes. Allow the roux to cool for a few minutes; blend
in the sour cream and beaten eggs. Add the sour cream mixture to
the chopped spinach and mix thoroughly.

Preheat oven to 375°F (190°C). Fill the onion cups with the combined spinach mixture and place the cups in a shallow baking pan.
Bake, uncovered, for 20 minutes. Serve at once.

**Serves 8**

# Grilled Onions

*Try these the next time you barbecue a steak!*

| | |
|---|---|
| 1 | Spanish onion per person |
| | Salt and pepper to taste |
| | Butter |

Soak whole, unpeeled onions in salted water for 1 hour. Place onions directly on a hot grill and cook, turning frequently, until skin is evenly black, about 30 minutes or until fork pierces the skin easily. Pull back outside skin and serve with salt, pepper and butter.

# Buttered Cognac Carrots

*An elegant way to serve carrots.*

| | | | |
|---|---|---|---|
| ¼ | cup butter | 50 | mL |
| 4 | teaspoons white sugar | 20 | mL |
| | Salt and pepper to taste | | |
| 1½ | pounds baby carrots, peeled | 750 | g |
| ¼ | cup Cognac | 50 | mL |
| | Parsley, chopped | | |

Preheat oven to 350°F (180°C). Combine butter, sugar, salt and pepper in a baking dish. Place in oven until butter is melted. Roll carrots in melted mixture until coated. Sprinkle with Cognac and bake, covered tightly, for 45 minutes or until tender. Garnish with parsley.
**Serves 4**

# Cold Carrots in Garlic

*Wonderful to munch on!*

| | | |
|---|---|---|
| 1 | large bunch carrots | 1 |
| 2 | garlic cloves, minced | 2 |
| ½ | teaspoon salt | 2 mL |
| ¼ | cup olive oil | 50 mL |
| 2 | tablespoons wine vinegar | 30 mL |
| 1 | teaspoon oregano | 5 mL |
| ½ | teaspoon black pepper | 2 mL |
| 1 | teaspoon basil | 5 mL |

Peel and slice carrots on the bias about ½ inch (1 cm) thick. Blanch carrots in boiling water for approximately 3 minutes. Drain and quickly run under cold water until cooled and still crunchy. Mix remaining ingredients together and beat or shake thoroughly. Pour over carrots and allow to marinate in the refrigerator for at least a day—two days is even better!

**Serves 6**

# Sunshine Carrots

*They gleam with an orange-ginger glaze.*

| | | |
|---|---|---|
| 5 | medium carrots, diagonally cut into 1-inch (2.5-cm) slices | 5 |
| 2 | teaspoons sugar | 10 mL |
| 1 | teaspoon cornstarch | 5 mL |
| ¼ | teaspoon salt | 1 mL |
| 1 | teaspoon freshly grated ginger (or ¼ teaspoon/1 mL ground ginger) | 5 mL |
| ¼ | cup orange juice | 50 mL |
| 2 | tablespoons butter | 30 mL |

Cook carrots in boiling, salted water just until tender, about 15 minutes. Drain. Meanwhile, combine sugar, cornstarch, salt and ginger in a small saucepan. Add orange juice and cook, stirring constantly, until mixture thickens and bubbles. Boil for 1 minute. Stir in butter. Pour over hot carrots, tossing to coat evenly.

**Serves 4**

# Fresh Green Beans with Almonds and Cherry Tomatoes

| | | | |
|---|---|---|---|
| 1½ | pounds green beans | 750 | g |
| 2-3 | tablespoons olive oil | 30-45 | mL |
| ½ | cup slivered almonds, toasted | 125 | mL |
| 1 | cup cherry tomatoes | 250 | mL |
| | Pinch of sugar or | | |
| 1 | teaspoon balsamic vinegar | 5 | mL |
| | Salt and freshly ground pepper | | |

Wash beans and cut tips off on the diagonal. Place in a large saucepan of boiling water. Boil 2 to 3 minutes until tender-crisp. Young tender beans take less time. Remove and rinse under cold water to stop cooking process. Drain and pat dry. This can be prepared early in the day. Refrigerate.

Just before serving time, heat olive oil in large fry pan. Sauté beans 2-3 minutes. Add almonds and cherry tomatoes. Sprinkle with sugar or stir in balsamic vinegar. Sauté 1-2 minutes more. Season to taste with salt and freshly ground pepper.

**Serves 6**

# Hot Bean Pot

*Absolutely "uncanny" how good this is!*

| | | |
|---|---|---|
| 1 | can (14 oz/398 mL) kidney beans | 1 |
| 1 | can (14 oz/398 mL) chick peas or lupini beans | 1 |
| 1 | can (14 oz/398 mL) green beans | 1 |
| 1 | can (14 oz/398 mL) yellow beans | 1 |
| 1 | can (14 oz/398 mL) pork and beans in molasses sauce | 1 |
| ½ | pound chopped bacon, browned and drained | 250 g |
| 4 | large onions, cut in rings | 4 |
| 2 | garlic cloves, minced | 2 |
| ½-1 | cup brown sugar | 125-250 mL |
| 2 | tablespoons molasses | 30 mL |
| 2 | teaspoons dry mustard | 10 mL |
| ½ | cup vinegar | 125 mL |

Preheat oven to 350°F (180°C). In a fry pan, brown bacon and remove. Cook onions and garlic in some of the bacon fat until soft and remove. Add sugar, molasses, mustard, and vinegar to pan. Simmer for 20 minutes. Add beans, bacon, onions and garlic. Mix and place in a 2½-quart (2.5-L) casserole and bake for 1 hour.
**Serves 12-14**

# Green Tomato Casserole

*Simplicity itself—a late summer must!*

| 4 | large green tomatoes, sliced | 4 |
|---|---|---|
|   | Salt and pepper to taste | |
| ¾ | cup Cheddar cheese, grated | 175 mL |
| 1 | tablespoon butter | 15 mL |

Preheat oven to 400°F (200°C). Butter a casserole dish. Lay ⅓ of the tomato slices on the bottom. Sprinkle with salt, pepper and ¼ cup (50 mL) cheese. Repeat with remaining slices. Top with ½ cup (125 mL) cheese and dot with butter. Bake covered for 40 minutes to 1 hour. Brown under broiler if you wish.
**Serves 4**

# Cheesy Cauliflower

*Serve ringed by sautéed cherry tomatoes and snow peas—spectacular!*

| 1 | head cauliflower, trimmed but left whole | 1 |
|---|---|---|
|   | Salt to taste | |
| ½ | cup mayonnaise | 125 mL |
| 2 | teaspoons Dijon mustard | 10 mL |
| ¾ | cup old Cheddar cheese, shredded | 175 mL |

Preheat oven to 375°F (190°C). Cook cauliflower in boiling, salted water until crisp tender, about 15 minutes. Drain and place in a shallow baking dish. Combine mayonnaise and mustard. Spread over cauliflower. Cover with cheese. Bake for approximately 10 minutes or until cheese is melted.
**Serves 6-8**

# Puffed Broccoli

*This can be served as a vegetable accompaniment or a luncheon or supper entrée.*

| | | | |
|---|---|---|---|
| ¼ | cup onion, chopped | 50 | mL |
| ¼ | cup butter | 50 | mL |
| 2 | tablespoons flour | 30 | mL |
| ½ | teaspoon dry mustard (or 1 teaspoon/5 mL Dijon mustard) | 2 | mL |
| ½ | cup water | 125 | mL |
| ½ | cup milk | 125 | mL |
| 1½ | cups grated sharp Cheddar cheese (or combination of crumbled Stilton or Gorgonzola and grated Cheddar) | 375 | mL |
| 1 | bunch fresh broccoli, blanched, drained and chopped (or 1 package [10 oz/300 g] frozen broccoli, thawed and chopped) | 1 | |
| 3 | eggs, separated | 3 | |
| ⅓ | cup bread crumbs | 75 | mL |
| | Sprinkling of Parmesan | | |

Preheat oven to 300°F (150°C). In a large saucepan, sauté onions in butter. Add flour, mustard, water and milk, and cook until mixture thickens. Add cheese and stir until melted. Remove from heat and cool to warm. Meanwhile, beat egg yolks. Add well-drained broccoli and yolks to cheese mixture. Beat egg whites until stiff and fold into cheese mixture. Place in a greased casserole. Top with bread crumbs and Parmesan. Place casserole in a pan of hot water and bake for 45 minutes with a lid on. Uncover and bake 15 minutes more.

**Serves 6**

# Scalloped Mushrooms and Almonds

*Bake in a pastry shell for a delicious luncheon dish!*

| | | | |
|---|---|---|---|
| 3 | pounds small, fresh mushrooms, cleaned | 1.5 | kg |
| ½ | cup butter | 125 | mL |
| 2 | cups 10% cream or milk | 500 | mL |
| 4 | tablespoons flour | 60 | mL |
| ¼ | cup water | 50 | mL |
| ⅓ | cup slivered almonds, toasted | 75 | mL |
| | Salt and pepper to taste | | |
| | Parsley and paprika | | |

Preheat oven to 350°F (180°C). In a large pot, cook mushrooms in butter for about 5 minutes. Do not brown. Add cream or milk and bring to a boil. Make a paste with the flour and water; stir into the mushroom mixture. Simmer for a few minutes to thicken. Add almonds, salt and pepper and pour into a casserole. Sprinkle with parsley and paprika. Bake until hot and brown, about 30 minutes.
**Serves 6-8**

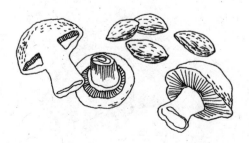

# Double Cheese Spinach

*A delicious way to serve spinach and have it completely ready ahead of time!*

| | | |
|---|---|---|
| 2 | packages (each 12 oz/340 g) frozen spinach, thawed, chopped and well drained | 2 |
| 4 | cups regular or light cottage cheese | 1 L |
| ¼ | pound Cheddar cheese, cut in small cubes | 125 g |
| 4 | tablespoons butter, softened | 60 mL |
| 3 | eggs, beaten | 3 |
| ¼ | teaspoon salt | 1 mL |
| 3 | tablespoons flour | 45 mL |

Preheat oven to 350°F (180°C). Place all ingredients, except flour, in a large bowl and mix well. Sprinkle flour over the mixture and blend well. Turn into a buttered 7" × 11" (3 L) baking dish. Bake about 1 hour or until set.

**Serves 8**

# Potatoes Romanoff

*Make a day ahead and relax!*

| | | | |
|---|---|---|---|
| 6 | good-sized potatoes | 6 | |
| 1½ | cups sharp Cheddar cheese, shredded | 375 | mL |
| 1 | bunch green onions, chopped | 1 | |
| 1½ | teaspoons salt | 7 | mL |
| ¼ | teaspoon pepper | 1 | mL |
| 2 | cups sour cream (not low fat)* | 500 | mL |
| | Paprika to taste | | |

Cook potatoes in jackets until tender. Peel and shred into a large buttered casserole. Gently stir in 1 cup (250 mL) cheese, onions, sour cream, salt and pepper. Top with remaining cheese. Sprinkle with paprika. Cover and refrigerate for several hours or overnight. Preheat oven to 350°F (180°C). Bake, uncovered, for about 30-40 minutes. **Serves 8-10**

*We tested this recipe with low-fat sour cream but found that it separates.

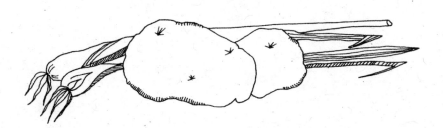

# Rosemary Potatoes

*Easy enough for family—good enough for company!*

| 6 | medium baking potatoes | 6 |
|---|---|---|
| 3-6 | tablespoons olive oil | 45-90 mL |
| | Salt and freshly ground pepper to taste | |
| | Generous pinch of dried rosemary, | |
| | finely crumbled | |

Preheat oven to 400°F (200°C). Scrub potatoes and cut into ¼-inch (1-cm) slices. Spread on paper towels to remove starch. Coat large baking sheet with half of the oil. Spread potatoes on sheet, overlapping only slightly. Brush remaining oil on potatoes; sprinkle with salt, pepper and rosemary. Bake until crisp on outside, tender on inside and golden brown, about 35-40 minutes.

**Serves 6**

# Jean's Hash Browns

*Perfect for a barbecue or a buffet.*

| 1 | package (2 pounds/1 kg) frozen hash brown potatoes | 1 |
|---|---|---|
| 1½ | cups sour cream | 375 mL |
| 2½ | cups Cheddar cheese, shredded and divided | 625 mL |
| 6 | slices bacon, cut in bite-sized pieces | 6 |
| 1 | pound fresh mushrooms, sliced | 500 g |
| 1 | large onion, chopped | 1 |
|  | Lots of freshly ground black pepper |  |

Preheat oven to 350°F (180°C). In a large bowl, mix together hash browns, sour cream and half of the Cheddar cheese. Pan-fry the bacon bits, adding the mushrooms and then the onions until cooked. Add these ingredients to the mixing bowl; sprinkle liberally with pepper and gently mix together. Place all ingredients in a well-greased large lasagne casserole dish. Sprinkle remaining cheese on top and bake for 30-40 minutes.

**Serves 10-12**

# Roasted Root Vegetables

| | | | |
|---|---|---|---|
| 3 | tablespoons olive oil | 45 | mL |
| 1-3 | garlic cloves, minced | 1-3 | |
| 2 | sweet potatoes or yams, peeled and quartered | 2 | |
| 4-6 | parsnips, peeled and cut in chunks | 4-6 | |
| 4-6 | carrots, peeled and cut in chunks | 4-6 | |
| 2 | onions, peeled and quartered | 2 | |
| 2 | medium potatoes, scrubbed and quartered | 2 | |
| | Salt and freshly ground pepper to taste | | |
| 3 | fresh rosemary sprigs, leaves only or | 3 | |
| 1 | teaspoon dried rosemary, crumbled | 5 | mL |

Preheat oven to 400°F (200°C). Place oil and garlic in a large heavy plastic bag. Add prepared vegetables and toss to distribute oil. Allow to marinate for 15 minutes or more. Spread vegetables, except sweet potatoes, on a greased, foil-lined baking sheet. Season with salt, pepper and rosemary. Bake for approximately 15 minutes, then add sweet potatoes and continue baking for an additional 25 minutes, or until vegetables are tender.
Serves 6-8

**TIP:** Vary the type and proportion of the vegetables to suit your own taste.

# Russian Noodles

*A dish fit for the Czar!*

| | | | |
|---|---|---|---|
| 8 | ounces thin noodles, cooked al dente, rinsed in cold water and drained | 250 | g |
| 1 | cup sour cream, regular or light | 250 | mL |
| 1 | cup plain yogourt, low fat | 250 | mL |
| 1 | small onion, grated | 1 | |
| 2 | teaspoons Worcestershire sauce | 10 | mL |
| ½ | teaspoon salt | 2 | mL |
| ¼ | teaspoon white pepper | 1 | mL |
| | Dash of Tabasco | | |
| 1 | cup sharp Cheddar cheese, grated and mixed with | 250 | mL |
| ½ | cup Parmesan cheese, grated | 125 | mL |

Preheat oven to 350°F (180°C). Mix all seasonings with sour cream and yogourt. Gently fold in noodles. Place in a buttered 9" × 13" (3.5 L) baking dish. Top with mixed cheeses. Bake, uncovered, for 25 minutes until bubbly.

**Serves 8**

**AN ADDED TOUCH:** Add 1 teaspoon (5 mL) or more poppy seeds to mixed cheeses if serving with beef or chicken. Mix 1 teaspoon (5 mL) crushed caraway seeds to mixed cheeses if serving with ham or pork.

# Wild Rice and Mushrooms

*Wild rice is worth a splurge every once in a while!*

| | | | |
|---|---|---|---|
| 1 | cup wild rice, well washed | 250 | mL |
| 1 | can (10 oz/284 mL) chicken broth, diluted with | 1 | |
| 1 | can of water | 1 | |
| 2 | tablespoons olive oil | 30 | mL |
| ½ | pound fresh mushrooms, sliced | 250 | g |
| 2 | medium onions, chopped | 2 | |
| 1 | teaspoon salt | 5 | mL |
| | Pinch of oregano, sage, marjoram and thyme | | |
| ½ | cup blanched, slivered almonds | 125 | mL |

Preheat oven to 350°F (180°C). Combine rice, broth and water in a large, heavy saucepan and simmer, covered, for about 45 minutes or until some grains have popped and rice is tender but not mushy. Add a bit more liquid if necessary during cooking time. Sauté mushrooms and onions in oil. Stir into rice and add all other ingredients, mixing well. Can be served immediately or reheated later.

**Serves 6**

# Barley and Mushroom Casserole

*A versatile and satisfying substitute for potatoes.*

| | | | |
|---|---|---|---|
| 3 | tablespoons butter or olive oil | 45 | mL |
| ½ | cup onion, chopped | 125 | mL |
| ½ | cup celery, diced | 125 | mL |
| ½ | pound fresh mushrooms, sliced | 250 | g |
| ½ | cup pearl or pot barley | 125 | mL |
| 3 | cups chicken or beef bouillon | 750 | mL |
| ¼ | cup slivered almonds | 50 | mL |

Preheat oven to 350°F (180°C). Sauté onions, celery and mushrooms in butter or oil until barely soft. Add barley and brown lightly. Add bouillon and almonds; heat until bubbly. If desired, season with salt and pepper. Pour into a casserole, cover and bake for 30 minutes. Uncover and continue baking until the liquid is completely absorbed, at least 30 minutes more.

**Serves 6**

# Breads

# German Dark Rye Bread

*Make in slim French sticks and slice thinly to serve with pâté or antipasto.*

| | | |
|---|---|---|
| 1 | package dry yeast | 1 |
| 2 | teaspoons sugar | 10 mL |
| 1 | cup lukewarm water | 250 mL |
| 2 | cups hot, strong coffee | 500 mL |
| ¼ | cup butter or shortening | 50 mL |
| ½-⅔ | cup molasses | 125-150 mL |
| 3 | teaspoons salt | 15 mL |
| 4 | cups dark rye flour | 1 L |
| 5 | cups all-purpose flour | 1.25 L |

Dissolve sugar in lukewarm water. Sprinkle yeast on top. Do not stir. Let stand in a warm place for 20 minutes. Pour coffee into a large mixing bowl. Add butter or shortening, molasses and salt. Stir until butter or shortening melts. Allow to cool to lukewarm. Beat in 2 cups (500 mL) rye flour, then yeast mixture and 2 cups (500 mL) all-purpose flour. Beat vigorously by hand or electric mixer. Then gradually beat in remaining flours, working the last in by hand. Turn dough onto a floured board and knead until elastic and smooth. Shape into a smooth ball and place in a greased bowl. Rotate the ball to grease all surfaces. Cover with a tea towel and let rise in a warm place until 1½ times original size, about 1½ hours.

Punch down and shape into 3 loaves or shape into French sticks. Place loaves in greased loaf pans, 8½" × 4½" (1.5 L) or put French sticks on greased baking sheets. Cover and allow to rise until 1½ times original size, about 1 hour.

Preheat oven to 375°F (190°C). Bake for 30-35 minutes or until loaves sound hollow when tapped.

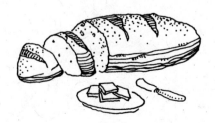

# Gooooood Bread!

*High in fibre, tops in taste!*

| | | | |
|---|---|---|---|
| ¼ | cup lukewarm water | 50 | mL |
| 1 | teaspoon sugar | 5 | mL |
| 4 | teaspoons dry yeast | 20 | mL |
| 2 | cups buttermilk, scalded* | 500 | mL |
| ¼ | cup butter | 50 | mL |
| 3 | tablespoons molasses, honey or sugar | 45 | mL |
| ⅛ | teaspoon baking soda | 0.5 | mL |
| 2 | teaspoons salt | 10 | mL |
| ½ | cup tofu, crumbled—optional | 125 | mL |
| 1 | egg, slightly beaten | 1 | |
| ⅓ | cup pepitas (Mexican pumpkin seeds), chopped | 75 | mL |
| ⅓ | cup sunflower seeds, whole or chopped | 75 | mL |
| ¼ | cup sesame seeds | 50 | mL |
| 2 | tablespoons poppy seeds | 30 | mL |
| 2 | tablespoons wheat germ | 30 | mL |
| ¼ | cup natural bran | 50 | mL |
| ¼ | cup rolled oats | 50 | mL |
| 1 | cup dark rye flour | 250 | mL |
| 1 | cup whole wheat flour | 250 | mL |
| 3-4 | cups white all-purpose flour | 750 mL-1 | L |

Mix water and sugar together. Sprinkle yeast on top and let stand in a warm place for 20 minutes. Meanwhile, scald milk and stir in butter, molasses, soda and salt. Allow to cool to lukewarm, then stir in tofu, egg and yeast mixture. Add seeds, wheat germ, bran, oats, rye flour and whole wheat flour. Add enough white flour to form a dough which can be handled. Turn out onto a floured board and knead 200 times. Form into a ball and place into a greased mixing bowl. Grease top of ball. Cover with a dry towel and allow to rise in a warm place until almost double in volume. Punch down. Let rest for 10 minutes.

Preheat oven to 375°F (190°C). Form dough into 2 large loaves and place in greased 9" × 5" (2 L) loaf pans. Cover and allow to rise until almost double in volume. Bake for 35-45 minutes or until loaves sound hollow when tapped. Turn out of pans and cool on a rack.
**Makes 2 large loaves**

**\*TIP:** If milk is substituted for buttermilk, eliminate the baking soda.

# French Onion Bread

*A pungent and sustaining bread. Try it with soup on a blustery winter night.*

| | | |
|---|---|---|
| 1 | package active dry yeast or | 1 |
| | 1 cake compressed yeast | |
| ¼ | cup water | 50 mL |
| 1 | envelope onion soup mix | 1 |
| 2 | cups water | 500 mL |
| 2 | tablespoons sugar | 30 mL |
| 2 | teaspoons salt | 10 mL |
| 2 | tablespoons Parmesan cheese, grated | 30 mL |
| 2 | tablespoons shortening or oil | 30 mL |
| 6-6½ | cups flour, sifted | 1.5-1.625 L |
| | Corn meal | |
| 1 | egg white | 1 |
| 1 | tablespoon water | 15 mL |

Soften dry yeast in ¼ cup (50 mL) warm water. Let stand in a warm place 15-20 minutes. Combine soup and second amount of water and simmer, covered, for 10 minutes. Add sugar, salt, cheese and shortening; stir. Cool to lukewarm and stir in 2 cups (500 mL) of flour; beat well. Stir in yeast. Add enough of the remaining flour to make a moderately stiff dough. Turn out on a lightly floured surface. Cover and let rest for 10 minutes. Knead until smooth and elastic, 8-10 minutes. Place in a lightly greased bowl and turn dough to grease surface. Cover and let stand in a warm place until double in size, 1¼-1½ hours. Punch down and divide in half. Cover and let rest 10 minutes. Shape into 2 long loaves, tapering ends. Place on a greased baking sheet and sprinkle with corn meal. Gash tops diagonally ¼ inch (0.5 cm) deep. Cover and let stand until almost double, about 1 hour.

Preheat oven to 375°F (190°C). Bake for 20 minutes. Brush the top with a mixture of 1 egg white and 1 tablespoon (15 mL) water. Bake 10-15 minutes longer or until done.

**Makes 2 loaves**

# Beer Bread

*Fantastic!*

| 3 | cups self-rising flour | 750 | mL |
| 1 | egg | 1 | |
| 2 | tablespoons sugar | 30 | mL |
| 1 | bottle (12 oz/341 mL) of beer, at room temperature | 1 | |

Preheat oven to 350°F (180°C). Beat egg, beer and sugar. Mix in flour. The batter will be sticky. Bake in a greased 9" × 5" (2 L) loaf pan for one hour.

**Makes 1 loaf**

# Easy Crusty French Bread

*Who could resist French bread?*

| 1 | package dry yeast | 1 | |
| 2 | cups warm water | 500 | mL |
| 4 | cups instant-blending or all-purpose flour | 1 | L |
| 3 | teaspoons sugar | 15 | mL |
| 2 | teaspoons salt | 10 | mL |

Dissolve 1 teaspoon (5 mL) sugar in ½ cup (125 mL) of the water. Sprinkle yeast on top and let stand 10 to 15 minutes until foamy. Measure flour, salt and remaining sugar into a large bowl. Add yeast mixture and remaining water to hold dough together. Mix until soft and sticky. Cover with a cloth and set in a warm place to rise until double in bulk, about 1 hour. Beat down and knead gently on a floured board for 1 minute. Roll into a rectangle with rolling pin, cut in half and shape into 2 French sticks. Place on a greased baking sheet and let rise about 1 hour or until double. Brush top with melted butter. Bake in a 350°F (180°C) oven for 35 minutes or until loaves sound hollow when tapped.

**Makes 2 loaves**

# Rhubarb Bread

| | | |
|---|---|---|
| 1½ | cups brown sugar | 375 mL |
| ⅔ | cup oil | 150 mL |
| 1 | egg | 1 |
| 1 | cup milk, soured with | 250 mL |
| | 1 tablespoon (15 mL) vinegar | |
| 1 | teaspoon salt | 5 mL |
| 1 | teaspoon baking soda | 5 mL |
| 1 | teaspoon vanilla | 5 mL |
| 2½ | cups flour | 625 mL |
| 1½ | cups fresh rhubarb, diced | 375 mL |
| ½ | cup nuts, chopped | 125 mL |

**TOPPING**

| | | |
|---|---|---|
| ½ | cup brown sugar | 125 mL |
| 1 | tablespoon butter | 15 mL |

Preheat oven to 350°F (180°C). Mix bread ingredients in order given. Pour into 1 large or 2 small greased loaf pans. Mix butter and sugar together to form topping and sprinkle over top of batter. Bake about 1 hour. Do not over bake.

**Makes 1 large or 2 small loaves**

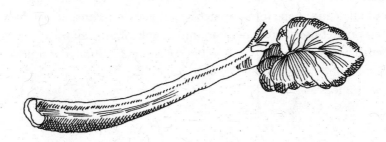

# Carrot Bread

*Good texture and flavour in this easy-to-make loaf.*

| | | | |
|---|---|---|---|
| 1 | cup white sugar | 250 | mL |
| 1¼ | cups corn oil | 300 | mL |
| 4 | eggs | 4 | |
| 3 | cups flour | 750 | mL |
| 2 | teaspoons baking powder | 10 | mL |
| 1½ | teaspoons baking soda | 7 | mL |
| ¼ | teaspoon salt | 1 | mL |
| 2 | teaspoons cinnamon | 10 | mL |
| 2 | cups carrots, finely shredded | 500 | mL |

Preheat oven to 350°F (180°C). Cream oil and sugar. Add eggs one at a time, beating well after each. Blend in dry ingredients, then fold in carrots. Bake in a greased 9" × 5" (2 L) loaf pan for about 1½ hours. Cool on a rack. This loaf freezes well.

**Makes 1 large loaf**

# Bran Bread

*Try it with chopped prunes or dates!*

| | | |
|---|---|---|
| ½-1 | cup brown sugar, lightly packed | 125-250 mL |
| 2 | cups bran | 500 mL |
| 2 | cups flour, sifted | 500 mL |
| 1 | teaspoon salt | 5 mL |
| 2 | teaspoons baking soda | 10 mL |
| 2 | cups buttermilk or sour cream | 500 mL |
| 1 | cup raisins | 250 mL |
| ½ | cup nuts, chopped | 125 mL |

Preheat oven to 350°F (180°C). Mix sugar, bran, flour, baking soda and salt. Add buttermilk or sour cream and mix well. Stir in raisins and nuts. Put mixture into greased 9" × 5" (2 L) loaf pan and bake for 1 hour. Cool and turn onto rack. Freezes well.

**Makes 1 loaf**

# Banana Blueberry Bread

*A refreshing variation on banana bread.*

| | | |
|---|---|---|
| 1½ | cups flour | 375 mL |
| ⅔ | cup sugar | 150 mL |
| 2 | teaspoons baking powder | 10 mL |
| ½ | teaspoon salt | 2 mL |
| ¾ | cup quick-cooking oats | 175 mL |
| ⅓ | cup salad oil | 75 mL |
| 2 | eggs, slightly beaten | 2 |
| 1 | cup bananas, mashed | 250 mL |
| ¾ | cup blueberries, fresh or frozen | 175 mL |

Preheat oven to 350°F (180°C). Sift first 4 ingredients together. Add oats, oil, eggs and bananas. Stir just enough to mix. Fold in blueberries lightly. Bake in a greased 9" × 5" (2 L) loaf pan for 1 hour. Cool in the pan for 10 minutes, then turn onto a wire rack. Wrap well when cool. Chill a few hours before slicing.

**Makes 1 loaf**

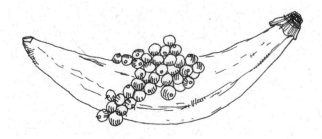

# Sour Cream Scones

*Serve hot from the oven with fresh preserves and whipped cream.*

| | | |
|---|---|---:|
| 2 | cups flour, sifted | 500 mL |
| ½ | teaspoon baking powder | 2 mL |
| ½ | teaspoon baking soda | 2 mL |
| ½ | teaspoon salt | 2 mL |
| 2 | tablespoons sugar plus a big pinch | 30 mL |
| ¼ | cup shortening | 50 mL |
| 2 | eggs | 2 |
| 1 | tablespoon lemon juice | 15 mL |
| 1 | teaspoon lemon rind, grated | 5 mL |
| ½ | cup thick sour cream, regular or no fat | 125 mL |
| 1 | tablespoon 10% cream | 15 mL |
| 1 | teaspoon sugar | 5 mL |

Preheat oven to 425°F (220°C). Sift first 5 ingredients together into a large bowl. Cut in shortening with a pastry blender. In a separate bowl, beat eggs, then add lemon juice, rind and sour cream. Combine the two mixtures and stir until the flour disappears. Knead in the bowl for 20 counts. Grease a pizza tray and roll or pat the dough on it to ½-inch (1 cm) thickness. Cut into 4 pie-shaped pieces, then cut each piece into 3, making 12 in all. Brush with cream and sprinkle lightly with sugar. Separate pieces slightly. Bake for 12-15 minutes. **Makes 12**

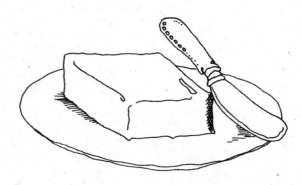

# Cottage Cheese Rolls

*Tastes like a yeast roll—good for breakfast or with soup.*

| | | | |
|---|---|---|---|
| 1 | cup cottage cheese, regular or light | 250 | mL |
| 1 | egg | 1 | |
| 3-4 | tablespoons milk or buttermilk | 45-60 | mL |
| 5 | tablespoons oil | 75 | mL |
| 2 | cups flour, sifted | 500 | mL |
| 1 | tablespoon baking powder | 15 | mL |
| $\frac{1}{8}$ | teaspoon baking soda, only if buttermilk is used | 0.5 | mL |
| 1 | teaspoon salt | 5 | mL |
| 1 | egg yolk | 1 | |

## OPTIONAL TOPPINGS
coarse salt, poppy seeds, caraway seeds

Preheat oven to 400°F (200°C). Blend cottage cheese, egg, milk and oil in food processor or by hand. Sift together dry ingredients and combine with cottage cheese mixture. Turn out onto a floured board and knead until smooth. Shape into 8 to 10 rolls and place on a greased cookie sheet. Brush each roll with undiluted egg yolk and slash the top with a knife. Sprinkle the tops with coarse salt, poppy seed or caraway seed—your choice. Bake for 20 minutes until golden. Serve warm.

**Makes 8-10**

# French Breakfast Puffs

*A heavenly treat for a Sunday breakfast.*

| | | | |
|---|---|---|---|
| ⅓ | cup soft shortening | 75 | mL |
| ½ | cup sugar | 125 | mL |
| 1 | egg | 1 | |
| 1½ | cups flour | 375 | mL |
| 1½ | teaspoons baking powder | 7 | mL |
| ½ | teaspoon salt | 2 | mL |
| ¼ | teaspoon nutmeg | 1 | mL |
| ½ | cup milk | 125 | mL |
| ¼ | cup butter | 50 | mL |
| ½ | cup sugar | 125 | mL |
| 1 | teaspoon cinnamon | 5 | mL |

Preheat oven to 350°F (180°C). Cream first 3 ingredients well. Sift together flour, baking powder, salt and nutmeg. Stir dry ingredients into creamed mixture alternately with milk. Grease small muffin tins well and fill ⅔ full. Bake for 20 minutes. While they are baking, melt butter in a small saucepan. Mix sugar and cinnamon together in a bowl. Dip hot puffs in melted butter, then roll in cinnamon and sugar mixture. Serve warm.

**Makes 2 dozen**

# Desserts

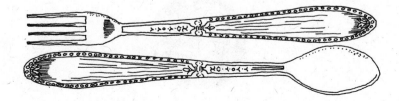

# Chocolate Coconut Tortoni

*Tortoni with a new twist!*

| | | |
|---|---|---|
| 2 | egg whites | 2 |
| ¼ | teaspoon cream of tartar | 1 mL |
| ¼ | cup sugar | 50 mL |
| 1½ | cups whipping cream | 375 mL |
| 1 | teaspoon vanilla | 5 mL |
| ¼ | cup orange liqueur | 50 mL |
| ¼ | cup toasted coconut | 50 mL |
| ⅓ | cup slivered almonds | 75 mL |
| 3 | squares (each 1 oz/28 g) semi-sweet chocolate, grated | 3 |

Beat egg whites and cream of tartar until light. Gradually beat in sugar until egg whites form stiff peaks. In separate bowl, beat cream until thick. Add orange liqueur and vanilla. Fold egg whites and cream together. Reserving ¼ for garnish, fold in coconut, almonds and chocolate. Pour into 8-inch (2-L) square pan. Freeze 4 hours or until firm. Garnish with reserved coconut, almonds and chocolate.
**Serves 8**

# Tortoni with Strawberries Cardinal

*Tortoni is also delicious on its own or served with other fruits.*

| 2 | egg yolks | 2 | |
|---|---|---|---|
| ½ | cup icing sugar | 125 | mL |
| ¾ | teaspoon almond extract | 4 | mL |
| 1 | cup whipping cream | 250 | mL |
| 2 | egg whites | 2 | |
| ¼ | teaspoon salt | 1 | mL |
| 5 | ounces slivered almonds, toasted and coarsely chopped | 150 | g |

In a small bowl, with a rotary beater or an electric mixer, beat egg yolks with sugar and almond extract until smooth and light. In a separate bowl, beat whipping cream until stiff. In a medium bowl with clean beaters, beat egg whites with salt until stiff. Gently fold egg yolk mixture and whipped cream into egg whites until well combined. Turn into a foil-lined ice cube tray. Cover and freeze until firm, 3-4 hours. Remove from tray and cut into 10 pieces. Press almonds into Tortoni to coat all sides. Return to freezer until serving time. Place Tortoni in individual serving dishes and top with Strawberries Cardinal (recipe follows). **Serves 10**

# Strawberries Cardinal

*Don't be afraid to use the sauce on fresh fruit, ice cream, plain cakes or puddings—it's wonderful!*

| 2 | quarts ripe, unblemished strawberries | 2 | L |
|---|---|---|---|
| 1 | package (15 oz/425 g) frozen raspberries | 1 | |
| ½ | cup sugar | 125 | mL |
| 2 | tablespoons Kirsch or Cointreau | 30 | mL |

Slice strawberries. Pass raspberries through a sieve. Blend raspberry purée, sugar and Kirsch in a blender for 2-3 minutes. Pour over strawberries. Chill.

# Strawberry Cracker Torte

*An easy, but very special dessert! Make it a day ahead.*

| | | |
|---|---|---|
| 3 | egg whites | 3 |
| ¾ | cup sugar | 175 mL |
| 1 | teaspoon vanilla | 5 mL |
| 1 | cup pecans, coarsely chopped | 250 mL |
| ¾ | cup soda crackers, finely crushed | 175 mL |
| 1 | quart strawberries, washed, drained and hulled | 1 L |
| 1 | tablespoon Grand Marnier | 15 mL |
| 1 | cup whipping cream | 250 mL |
| 1 | teaspoon vanilla | 5 mL |
| 1 | tablespoon sugar | 15 mL |

Preheat oven to 325°F (160°C). Beat egg whites in a bowl until they hold soft peaks. Add sugar a little at a time. Add vanilla and continue to beat until mixture is stiff. Fold in pecans and cracker crumbs. Spread in a buttered 9" (1 L) pie plate, building up sides. Bake for 30-35 minutes or until lightly browned. Cool completely. Fill with hulled strawberries; drizzle with Grand Marnier. Whip the cream and flavour with vanilla and sugar. Spread over the berries. Chill, covered, at least 8 hours or overnight. Garnish with berries and serve. This recipe doubles easily. Bake doubled mixture in a circle on a lightly greased cookie sheet.

**Serves 8**

# Bavarian Apple Torte

*One of the world's best apple desserts!*

## BASE

| | | | |
|---|---|---|---|
| ½ | cup butter | 125 | mL |
| ⅓ | cup sugar | 75 | mL |
| ¼ | teaspoon vanilla | 1 | mL |
| 1 | cup flour | 250 | mL |
| ¼ | cup raspberry jam | 50 | mL |

## FILLING

| | | | |
|---|---|---|---|
| 8 | ounces cream cheese, regular or light block-style | 250 | g |
| ¼ | cup sugar | 50 | mL |
| 1 | egg | 1 | |
| ½ | teaspoon vanilla | 2 | mL |

## TOPPING

| | | | |
|---|---|---|---|
| ⅓ | cup sugar | 75 | mL |
| ½ | teaspoon cinnamon | 2 | mL |
| 4 | cups apples, peeled, cored and sliced | 1 | L |
| ½ | cup almonds, sliced | 125 | mL |

Preheat oven to 450°F (230°C). To make crust, cream butter, sugar and vanilla. Blend in flour. Press on the bottom and sides of a 9" (2 L) springform pan. Spread with a thin layer of raspberry jam.

For the filling, combine the cream cheese and sugar. Add the egg and vanilla; mix well. Pour over jam.

For the topping, toss the apples with the sugar and cinnamon and spoon over the cream cheese mixture. Sprinkle with almonds. Bake at 450°F (230°C) for 10 minutes, then 400°F (200°C) for 25 minutes. Cool and carefully remove sides of pan. Store in a cool place until needed.

**Serves 8-10**

# Walnut Torte

*A delicious dessert that must be made a day in advance.*

| ½ | cup butter | 125 mL |
|---|---|---|
| 1¼ | cups sugar | 300 mL |
| ½ | teaspoon vanilla | 2 mL |
| 4 | eggs, separated | 4 |
| 1 | cup flour, sifted | 250 mL |
| | Dash of salt | |
| 2 | teaspoons baking powder | 10 mL |
| ⅓ | cup milk | 75 mL |
| | Dash of cream of tartar | |
| ¾ | cup walnuts, finely hand chopped | 175 mL |

**CHOCOLATE CREAM**

| ⅓ | cup Dutch cocoa | 75 mL |
|---|---|---|
| 1½ | cups whipping cream | 375 mL |
| ½ | cup sugar | 125 mL |

Preheat oven to 300°F (150°C). Cream butter, ½ cup (125 mL) sugar and vanilla. Add yolks, one at a time and beat well after each. Sift flour, salt and baking powder together and add alternately with milk to butter mixture. Pour into 2 wax paper-lined 9" (1.5 L) round pans and set aside. Beat egg whites until stiff; add cream of tartar, then gradually add remaining ¾ cup (175 mL) sugar. Continue beating until glossy and sugar is dissolved. Fold in hand-chopped nuts and spread over cake batter. Bake for 1 hour. Cool completely, remove from pans and remove paper. The meringue will fall after baking.

For the chocolate cream, combine the cocoa, sugar and cream in a bowl, and refrigerate for at least 1 hour. Whip until stiff. Use to fill and frost torte. Refrigerate, covered, overnight.
**Serves 12**

**VARIATION:** Instead of chocolate cream, fill and frost with 1½ cups (375 mL) whipped cream mixed with ¾ cup (175 mL) well-drained crushed pineapple.

# Hazelnut Torte

*Quick, delicious and foolproof!*

## CAKE

| | | | |
|---|---|---|---|
| 4 | eggs | 4 | |
| ¾ | cup sugar | 175 | mL |
| 2 | tablespoons flour | 30 | mL |
| 2½ | teaspoons baking powder | 12 | mL |
| 1 | cup hazelnuts (or filberts!) | 250 | mL |

## MOCHA FILLING

| | | | |
|---|---|---|---|
| 2 | tablespoons soft butter | 30 | mL |
| 1 | cup icing sugar | 250 | mL |
| 2 | tablespoons strong, hot coffee | 30 | mL |
| 1 | teaspoon cocoa | 5 | mL |
| ½ | teaspoon vanilla | 2 | mL |

## TOPPING

| | | | |
|---|---|---|---|
| 1 | cup whipping cream | 250 | mL |
| 1 | teaspoon sugar | 5 | mL |
| 1 | tablespoon Tia Maria | 15 | mL |

Preheat oven to 350°F (180°C). In a blender, whirl eggs and sugar until well mixed. Add flour, baking powder and hazelnuts. Blend at high speed for a few seconds. Pour into two 8" (1.2 L) round pans, lined with waxed paper or cooking parchment. Bake for about 20 minutes, or until tester comes out clean. To make filling, cream butter and icing sugar; add coffee, vanilla and cocoa, and spread between cooled layers. Whip cream with sugar and Tia Maria; spread over top and sides of torte. Decorate with chocolate curls or serve with fresh fruit.

**Serves 8**

# Frozen Lemon Torte

*Expect raves and requests for the recipe!*

| | | | |
|---|---|---|---|
| 2 | packages lady fingers | 2 | |
| 5 | eggs, separated | 5 | |
| ¾ | cup fresh lemon juice | 175 | mL |
| | rind of 1 lemon, grated | | |
| 1¼ | cups sugar | 300 | mL |
| 2 | cups whipping cream, whipped* | 500 | mL |
| 4 | tablespoons icing sugar | 60 | mL |
| | Dash of cream of tartar | | |

Butter a 10" (3 L) springform pan and line sides and bottom with split lady fingers. In a saucepan, beat 5 egg yolks and 2 egg whites (reserve remaining whites) until thick. Add juice, rind and sugar. Cook over low heat until thickened. Let cool completely. Fold in the whipped cream and pour into the prepared pan. Freeze overnight, or at least 6 hours, covered with foil. Next day, beat the remaining 3 egg whites; add icing sugar and cream of tartar and beat until stiff. Spread over the frozen torte and place under the broiler until lightly browned. Watch carefully. Cool for a few minutes and return to the freezer until ready to use. Defrost 1½-2 hours in the refrigerator before serving.

**Serves 10**

**\*TIP:** Evaporated milk works well in place of the whipped cream and many actually prefer this version. To whip evaporated milk, place milk in mixing bowl. Put in freezer along with beaters and chill until ice crystals form around edges. Remove from freezer and beat until stiff peaks form. (Note: 2% evaporated milk will not whip.)

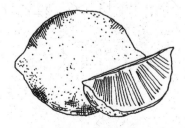

# Baked Lemon Pudding

*Perfect "oven meal" dessert.*

| | | | |
|---|---|---|---|
| 3 | eggs, separated | 3 | |
| 1½ | lemons, rind and juice | 1½ | |
| 2 | tablespoons flour | 30 | mL |
| ½ | cup sugar | 125 | mL |
| 1 | tablespoon butter, melted | 15 | mL |
| 1 | cup milk | 250 | mL |
| | Pinch of salt | | |

Preheat oven to 325°F (160°C). In a large bowl, combine rind and juice with egg yolks. Add flour and sugar slowly. Beat well and add milk and butter gradually. Beat egg whites until stiff and fold into mixture. Pour into greased, 1½-quart (1.5-L) casserole, and set in pan of warm water. Bake 45 minutes or until set and top is golden brown.
**Serves 6**

# Ricotta Torte

*Top with fruit yogourt and fresh fruit.*

| | | | |
|---|---|---|---|
| 4 | cups light or whole Ricotta cheese | 1 | L |
| 4 | medium eggs | 4 | |
| 1 | cup buttermilk | 250 | mL |
| ½ | cup brown sugar or honey | 125 | mL |
| 2 | teaspoons pure vanilla | 10 | mL |
| | Juice and rind of 1 lime or 1 lemon | | |
| ¼ | teaspoon salt | 1 | mL |

Preheat oven to 375°F (190°C). Combine all ingredients in blender. Purée until very smooth and well blended. Pour into lightly buttered 10-inch (3-L) springform pan and bake for 45 minutes next to a pan of water in the oven. Cool and serve.
**Serves 8-10**

# Caribbean Lime Pie

## COCONUT PIE CRUST

| | | | |
|---|---|---|---|
| 3 | cups sweetened coconut, shredded | 750 | mL |
| 5 | tablespoons butter, melted | 75 | mL |

## FILLING

| | | | |
|---|---|---|---|
| ½ | cup fresh lime juice | 125 | mL |
| 1 | envelope unflavoured gelatin | 7 | g |
| 5 | egg yolks | 5 | |
| 1 | cup sugar | 250 | mL |
| 3 | tablespoons light rum | 45 | mL |
| 1 | tablespoon Cointreau | 15 | mL |
| | Rind of 2 limes, grated | | |
| 5 | egg whites | 5 | |
| 1 | cup whipping cream, whipped | 250 | mL |
| 1 | cup whipping cream for garnishing, whipped | 250 | mL |
| | Lime slices for garnishing | | |

Preheat oven to 350°F (180°C). For the crust, spread coconut over bottom of jelly roll pan and toast lightly, about 7 minutes. Reserve ½ cup (125 mL) for garnish. Combine remaining coconut with melted butter. Toss until coconut is thoroughly coated. Press coconut mixture firmly into bottom and sides of **deep** 9" (1 L) pie plate or 10" (3 L) springform pan.

Cover lightly and refrigerate until firm. For the filling, soften gelatin in lime juice. Place over simmering water and heat until gelatin is completely liquified, 2 to 3 minutes. Meanwhile, combine egg yolks and ½ cup (125 mL) sugar in top of double boiler; beat with an electric mixer. Add gelatin mixture and continue beating until mixture is thick enough to leave a path when a finger is drawn across spoon, about 10 minutes. Remove mixture from heat and let cool. Blend in rum, Cointreau and lime peel. Beat egg whites until soft peaks form. With mixer at medium speed, gradually add remaining ½ cup (125 mL) sugar and beat until whites are stiff and glossy. Stir 1 heaping spoonful of egg white into cooled custard, mixing well. Gently fold custard into whites with large spatula, blending lightly to create marbleized effect. (Do not overfold.)

Gently fold in whipped cream. Spoon filling into crust, mounding and swirling in centre to create a dome shape in pie plate (smooth in springform pan). Refrigerate or freeze until firm. Just before serving, pipe rosettes over top of pie with remaining whipped cream. Garnish with lime slices and toasted coconut.

**Serves 12-16**

# Mud Pie

*Sin in a plate.*

| 1 | cup chocolate wafers (½ package), crushed | 250 | mL |
|---|---|---|---|
| ¼ | cup melted butter | 50 | mL |
| 4 | cups coffee or mocha ice cream | 1 L | |
| 1½ | cups fudge sauce | 375 | mL |
| 1 | cup whipping cream, whipped | 250 | mL |
| ¼ | cup slivered almonds, toasted | 50 | mL |

Crush wafers and add butter. Mix well and press into 9" (1 L) pie plate. Cover with soft ice cream and put into freezer until firm. Top with cold fudge sauce and store in freezer for approximately 10 hours. Slice mud pie into 6 or 8 portions. Serve on chilled plate with chilled fork. Top with whipped cream and slivered almonds.

If you can't find mocha ice cream, dissolve 1½ tablespoons (25 mL) instant coffee in 1 tablespoon (15 mL) water and mix it with chocolate ice cream.

**Serves 6-8**

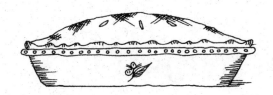

# Frozen Strawberry Meringue

*Easy, inexpensive and yummy!*

## CRUST

| | | | |
|---|---|---|---|
| 1 | cup graham cracker crumbs | 250 | mL |
| 3 | tablespoons sugar | 45 | mL |
| ¼ | cup butter or margarine, melted | 50 | mL |
| ½ | cup pecans, finely chopped | 125 | mL |

## FILLING

| | | | |
|---|---|---|---|
| 2 | cups fresh or drained frozen strawberries, sliced | 500 | mL |
| 1 | cup sugar | 250 | mL |
| 2 | egg whites | 2 | |
| 1 | tablespoon lemon juice | 15 | mL |
| 1 | teaspoon vanilla | 5 | mL |
| | Dash of salt | | |
| ½ | cup whipping cream | 125 | mL |

Preheat oven to 325°F (160°C). Combine cracker crumbs, sugar, butter and pecans. Press into the bottom of a 10" (3 L) springform pan. Bake for 10 minutes. Cool. Combine 2 cups (500 mL) of berries, sugar, egg whites, lemon juice, vanilla and salt in large bowl of mixer. Beat on low speed to blend, then on high speed until peaks form, about 15 minutes. In another bowl, beat cream until soft peaks form, then fold cream into berry mixture. Pour into cooled crust. Cover and freeze overnight. To serve, carefully remove sides of pan and garnish if desired.

**Serves 10-12**

# Strawberries Romanoff

*Sheer heaven!*

| | | | |
|---|---|---|---|
| 1 | quart fresh strawberries | 1 | L |
| 4 | tablespoons red currant jelly, melted | 60 | mL |
| | juice from 1 orange plus a little rind | | |
| 2-4 | tablespoons Cointreau, Triple Sec or Grand Marnier | 30-60 | mL |

Mix currant jelly with liqueur, orange juice and grated rind until smooth. Wash berries as quickly as possible, removing stems after they are washed. Spread berries to dry on paper towels. One half hour before serving, carefully mix the berries with sauce. Serve with whipped cream, ice cream or trifle.

**Serves 4-6**

# The Sting!

*Light airy dessert—don't serve to the teetotalers!*

| | | | |
|---|---|---|---|
| 1 | envelope (1 tablespoon/7 g) unflavoured gelatin | 1 | |
| 2 | tablespoons cold water | 30 | mL |
| 6 | tablespoons orange juice | 90 | mL |
| ½-1 | cup white sugar | 125-250 | mL |
| ⅓ | cup rum | 75 | mL |
| 2 | tablespoons rye | 30 | mL |
| 2 | egg whites | 2 | |
| 1 | cup whipping cream | 250 | mL |

Soak gelatin in cold water for 5 minutes. Heat orange juice. Add gelatin and stir until dissolved. Add sugar; stir to dissolve. Remove from heat. Stir in rum and rye. Refrigerate until thickened, about 2 hours. Beat until frothy (2-3 minutes). Beat egg whites until stiff but not dry. Fold into orange mixture. Beat whipping cream until stiff peaks form. Fold in. Cover and refrigerate until serving time. Decorate with chocolate curls.

**Serves 6**

# Overnight Winter Fruit Bowl

*An excellent, light dessert.*

| | | |
|---|---|---|
| 3 | egg yolks, beaten | 3 |
| 2 | tablespoons white sugar | 30 mL |
| 2 | tablespoons white vinegar | 30 mL |
| 2 | tablespoons pineapple juice or syrup from a can | 30 mL |
| 1 | tablespoon butter | 15 mL |
| | Salt to taste | |
| 2 | cups seeded grapes or drained pitted cherries | 500 mL |
| 2 | cups pineapple chunks, drained | 500 mL |
| 2 | cups mandarin oranges, drained | 500 mL |
| 2 | cups tiny marshmallows | 500 mL |
| 1 | cup whipping cream, whipped | 250 mL |

Combine the first six ingredients in a double boiler. Cook and stir until thick. *Do not boil!* Fold this cooled sauce into whipped cream, then fold into the fruit. Place in a large serving bowl and garnish the top with fruit if desired. Place in the refrigerator for 24 hours. Serve cold.

**Serves 8-10**

# Crème Caramel

*A beautiful tradition—always a hit!*

| | | | |
|---|---|---|---|
| 1 | cup fruit sugar | 250 | mL |
| 4 | cups whole milk | 1 | L |
| ⅔ | cup sugar | 150 | mL |
| 6 | eggs | 6 | |
| 2 | egg yolks | 2 | |
| 1½ | teaspoons vanilla | 7 | mL |

Preheat oven to 325°F (160°C). In a heavy-bottomed saucepan, melt fruit sugar over medium heat. Stir often and watch carefully as it will burn very quickly. When caramel is ready, pour into a hot, 2-quart (2-L) soufflé dish and rotate until bottom and sides are covered with caramel. Set aside. In another saucepan, heat the milk to just below the boiling point. While milk is heating, beat all the eggs and sugar with a whisk. Do not overbeat or the dessert will turn out bubbly. Pour the hot milk slowly into the egg mixture with vanilla. Pour into soufflé dish. Set this dish in a baking pan, filled halfway up with boiling water. Bake for 1 hour or until a pointed knife inserted in the centre comes out clean. The caramel is best done a day ahead. Cool in refrigerator and, at serving time, unmold into a deep-sided plate so you won't lose any of the lovely sauce!

**Serves 6-8**

# Gingerbread

*Try it with real maple syrup!*

| | | | |
|---|---|---|---|
| ¼ | cup shortening | 50 | mL |
| ¼ | cup butter | 50 | mL |
| ½ | cup brown sugar | 125 | mL |
| 1 | egg | 1 | |
| ½ | cup molasses | 125 | mL |
| 2 | cups cake and pastry flour | 500 | mL |
| ½ | teaspoon ginger | 2 | mL |
| ½ | teaspoon allspice | 2 | mL |
| ½ | teaspoon cinnamon | 2 | mL |
| ¼ | teaspoon salt | 1 | mL |
| 1 | teaspoon baking soda dissolved in ½ cup (125 mL) hot water | 5 | mL |

Preheat oven to 350°F (180°C). Cream butter and shortening; add sugar, then egg and molasses. Mix well. Sift flour, then measure two cups and sift again with spices and salt. Add to egg mixture alternately with hot water and soda mixture. Bake in a greased 8" (2 L) square pan for 25 to 30 minutes or until cake springs back to the touch of a finger. Serve warm with real maple syrup. Other sauces may be used, such as applesauce or lemon sauce.

**Serves 8**

# Chocolate Almond Mousse

*A silken smooth mousse with crunchy nuts—a five-star dessert!*

| | | |
|---|---|---|
| ¼ | cup sugar | 50 mL |
| ⅓ | cup water | 75 mL |
| 1 | cup whipping cream | 250 mL |
| 6 | squares (each 1 oz/28 g) semi-sweet chocolate | 6 |
| 3 | tablespoons dark rum | 45 mL |
| 3 | eggs, separated | 3 |
| ½ | cup blanched almonds, toasted | 125 mL |

Combine water and sugar in a small saucepan and boil for 3 minutes. Set aside. Using food processor with a metal blade, whip cream
until very thick. Transfer to a large bowl. Without washing work
bowl, process chocolate pieces, turning on and off for 15-20 seconds.
Continue processing and pour in hot syrup, rum and yolks. Add
almonds and process, turning on and off, until nuts are coarsely
chopped. Transfer chocolate mixture to bowl with cream; mix thoroughly. Beat egg whites until stiff and fold into chocolate mixture.
Spoon into individual glasses or a large bowl and chill until set.
Mousse may be frozen in a mold for 6 hours, unmolded and served.
**Serves 8-10**

# Rhubarb Mousse

*A taste treat for rhubarb lovers!*

| | | | |
|---|---|---|---|
| 4 | cups rhubarb, cut in 1-inch (2.5-cm) pieces | 1 | L |
| ¾ | cup sugar | 175 | mL |
| 1 | stick cinnamon | 1 | |
| 3 | tablespoons water | 45 | mL |
| 1 | envelope (1 tablespoon/7 g) gelatin | 1 | |
| ¼ | cup cold water | 50 | mL |
| 1 | cup whipping cream, whipped | 250 | mL |

Bring rhubarb, sugar, cinnamon and water to a boil and simmer for 20 minutes. Discard cinnamon stick. Remove ½ cup (125 mL) rhubarb with a slotted spoon and reserve. Purée the remaining rhubarb and juice in a blender. There should be 2 cups (500 mL). Dissolve gelatin in cold water and stir into rhubarb purée. Cool slightly until partially set. Fold reserved rhubarb pieces and whipped cream into purée. Pour into a 4-cup (1-L) mold, rinsed in cold water. Chill until set. Garnish with additional whipped cream, strawberries or kiwi fruit if desired.

**Serves 8**

# Pies, Cakes and Cookies

# Ontario Blue Grape Pie

*A show-stopper for autumn meals!*

| | | | |
|---|---|---|---|
| 1 | 9-inch (1-L) pie shell, unbaked | 1 | |
| 5 | cups stemmed Ontario Concord blue grapes | 1.25 | L |
| 2 | teaspoons lemon juice | 10 | mL |
| ¾-1 | cup white sugar | 175-250 | mL |
| 2 | tablespoons cornstarch | 30 | mL |
| ¼ | teaspoon salt | 1 | mL |
| ⅓ | cup flour | 75 | mL |
| 2 | tablespoons sugar | 30 | mL |
| 2 | tablespoons butter | 30 | mL |

Preheat oven to 425°F (220°C). Slip skins from grapes and reserve. Place pulp in saucepan and bring to a boil. Reduce heat and simmer 5 minutes. Sieve to remove seeds; stir in skins. Add the lemon juice. Mix sugar, cornstarch and salt together, and stir into the hot grape mixture. Pour into unbaked pie shell. Combine remaining ingredients. Sprinkle evenly over filling. Bake in preheated oven for 15 minutes. Reduce heat to 350°F (180°C) and continue baking 25-30 minutes. Cool before serving to allow filling to set. If desired, freeze the prepared filling for a winter taste treat!

**Serves 6**

# Pecan Kahlua Pie

*Worth every calorie!!*

| | | | |
|---|---|---|---|
| 1 | 9-inch (1-L) pie shell, unbaked | 1 | |
| ¼ | cup butter | 50 | mL |
| 1 | cup brown sugar | 250 | mL |
| 3 | eggs, at room temperature and well beaten | 3 | |
| ¼ | cup Kahlua or Tia Maria | 50 | mL |
| ¼ | cup light corn syrup | 50 | mL |
| 1½ | cups pecans, chopped | 375 | mL |
| 1 | tablespoon rum | 15 | mL |

Preheat oven to 375°F (190°C). Cream butter and sugar. Add well-beaten eggs and mix thoroughly. Add remaining ingredients and mix well. Pour into pie shell. Place on a cookie sheet and bake 35-40 minutes or until a knife inserted in the centre comes out clean. Serve with vanilla ice cream or whipped cream.

**Serves 8**

# Old-Time Lemon Meringue Pie

| | | |
|---|---|---|
| ¾ | cup white sugar | 175 mL |
| 1¼ | cups water | 300 mL |
| 1 | tablespoon butter | 15 mL |
| ¼ | cup cornstarch | 50 mL |
| 3 | tablespoons cold water | 45 mL |
| 3 | egg yolks | 3 |
| 2 | tablespoons milk | 30 mL |
| 6 | tablespoons fresh lemon juice | 90 mL |
| 1 | teaspoon grated lemon rind | 5 mL |
| 1 | 8-inch (1-L) pastry shell, baked and cooled | 1 |
| 3 | egg whites | 3 |
| 6 | tablespoons white sugar | 90 mL |
| 1 | teaspoon lemon juice | 5 mL |

Preheat oven to 350°F (180°C). In a medium saucepan, combine sugar, water and butter; heat until sugar dissolves. Blend cornstarch with cold water; add to hot mixture. Cook slowly until clear and thick, about 8 minutes. Beat egg yolks with milk; slowly stir into cornstarch mixture. Cook 2 minutes until it bubbles, stirring constantly. Remove from heat. Add lemon juice and grated rind. Cool. Pour into cooled baked pastry shell. Beat egg whites until stiff but not dry; add sugar gradually. Add 1 teaspoon (5 mL) lemon juice. Spread meringue over cooled filling, sealing to edges of pastry to avoid shrinking. Bake in oven 12-13 minutes until lightly browned. **Serves 6**

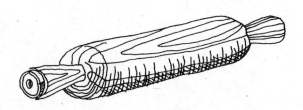

# Peach Sour Cream Pie

*Sour cream sparks the flavour of our wonderful Ontario peaches.*

| 1 | cup sour cream | 250 mL |
| | Juice of ½ orange and grated rind | |
| ½ | cup brown sugar | 125 mL |
| ¼ | teaspoon salt | 1 mL |
| 2 | egg yolks, well beaten | 2 |
| 5 | tablespoons flour | 75 mL |
| 2½ | cups fresh peaches, sliced | 625 mL |
| 1 | deep 8-inch (1.2-L) pie shell, unbaked | 1 |

Preheat oven to 425°F (220°C). Blend sour cream, orange juice, brown sugar and salt. Stir in egg yolks. Sprinkle pie shell with 2 tablespoons (30 mL) flour. Pour in peaches and sprinkle with remaining flour. Pour sour cream mixture over all. Bake at 425°F (220°C) for 15 minutes. Reduce heat to 350°F (180°C) and bake for 40 minutes more. Let cool and serve.

**Serves 6**

# Maple Syrup Tarts

| | | |
|---|---|---|
| ¼ | cup butter | 50 mL |
| ¾ | cup brown sugar | 175 mL |
| ½ | cup maple syrup | 125 mL |
| 2 | tablespoons milk | 30 mL |
| ¾ | cup raisins | 175 mL |
| 1 | egg, beaten | 1 |
| ½ | cup walnuts or pecans, chopped | 125 mL |
| ½ | cup fine coconut | 125 mL |
| 1 | teaspoon vanilla | 5 mL |
| | If desired, a little raspberry or strawberry jam | |
| | pastry for 12-16 tarts | |

Preheat oven to 400°F (200°C). Pour 1 teaspoon (5 mL) of maple
syrup, from the ½ cup (125 mL), into each pastry-lined tart tin. If
desired, add ½ teaspoon (2 mL) jam to each tart. Beat egg with
brown sugar; add remaining maple syrup. Add milk. Add softened
(but not melted) butter and mix well. Soak raisins for 2 minutes in
boiling water, drain and dry. Add raisins, walnuts, coconut and
vanilla. Mix. Spoon filling into tins, filling not more than ½ full.
Bake 20 minutes. If they threaten to boil over, after 10 minutes
reduce to 350°F (180°C) and continue cooking until pastry is brown.
**Makes 12 very large or 16 medium tarts**

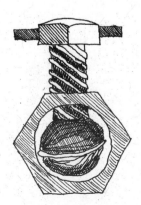

# Crumb Cake

*Great served for that get-together over coffee!*

| | | | |
|---|---|---|---|
| 1¾ | cups flour | 425 | mL |
| 1 | cup brown sugar | 250 | mL |
| ¾ | cup shortening | 175 | mL |
| ¼ | teaspoon salt | 1 | mL |
| ¼ | teaspoon nutmeg | 1 | mL |
| ¼ | teaspoon cloves | 1 | mL |
| 1 | teaspoon cinnamon | 5 | mL |
| 1 | egg | 1 | |
| ¾ | cup raisins | 175 | mL |
| ¾ | cup milk with | 175 | mL |
| | 1 tablespoon (15 mL) vinegar | | |
| ¼ | cup brown sugar | 50 | mL |
| 1 | teaspoon baking soda | 5 | mL |

Preheat oven to 350°F (180°C). Mix flour, brown sugar and shortening with fingers until crumbly. Set aside ¾ cup (175 mL) for topping. Add remaining ingredients and beat until smooth. Pour into greased 7" × 11" (3 L) pan. Sprinkle remaining crumbs over top. Bake for about 40 minutes.

**Serves 6-8**

# Chocolate Mocha Cake

*Kids love it and, moreover, it serves a crowd.*

| | | | |
|---|---|---|---|
| 2 | cups white sugar | 500 | mL |
| 2 | eggs | 2 | |
| 2 | teaspoons vanilla | 10 | mL |
| ⅔ | cup salad oil | 150 | mL |
| 2⅔ | cups all-purpose flour | 650 | mL |
| ⅔ | cup cocoa | 150 | mL |
| 2 | teaspoons baking soda | 10 | mL |
| 2 | teaspoons baking powder | 10 | mL |
| 1 | teaspoon salt | 5 | mL |
| 1 | teaspoon cinnamon | 5 | mL |
| 2 | cups boiling coffee | 500 | mL |

Preheat oven to 350°F (180°C). Beat sugar, eggs, vanilla and oil for 4 minutes. Combine dry ingredients and add alternately to egg mixture with coffee. Start and finish with dry ingredients. Pour into 9" × 13" (3.5 L) pan. Bake 40 to 50 minutes. Top with favourite chocolate icing.

**Serves 15-20**

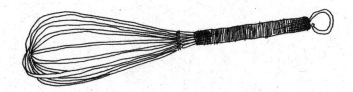

# Coconut Cake

*This is for coconut lovers!*

| | | | |
|---|---|---|---|
| 1 | pound butter | 500 | g |
| 2 | cups sugar | 500 | mL |
| 6 | eggs | 6 | |
| 2 | cups flour | 500 | mL |
| 1 | teaspoon almond flavouring | 5 | mL |
| 3 | cups shredded coconut | 750 | mL |
| 1 | orange, peeled and sliced | 1 | |
| 2 | tablespoons Grand Marnier | 30 | mL |

**GLAZE**

| | | | |
|---|---|---|---|
| 1 | cup sugar | 250 | mL |
| ½ | cup water | 125 | mL |
| 1 | teaspoon vanilla | 5 | mL |

Preheat oven to 375°F (190°C). Cream butter and sugar until fluffy;
add 1 cup (250 mL) of flour and mix well. Beat in the eggs, one at a
time until well blended. Add almond flavouring and stir. Mix
remaining cup (250 mL) of flour with the coconut; add to batter,
blending well. Bake in a greased 9" (2 L) tube pan for about 1 hour
or until tester comes out clean. About 15 minutes before cake is ready,
mix together sugar, water and vanilla and simmer for 10 minutes.
When cake is done, remove from pan and brush on all the glaze
while cake is still hot. Cover loosely with foil and let rest for at least
24 hours. Decorate serving plate with orange slices marinated in
Grand Marnier. Serve in thin slices. A bundt pan may also be used.
**Serves 12 or more**

# Almond Cake

*A treat for almond lovers!*

| | | | |
|---|---|---:|---|
| 1 | cup all-purpose flour | 250 | mL |
| ½ | cup white sugar | 125 | mL |
| ½ | teaspoon baking powder | 2 | mL |
| ½ | teaspoon baking soda | 2 | mL |
| ¼ | teaspoon salt | 1 | mL |
| 1 | egg | 1 | |
| ½ | cup buttermilk* | 125 | mL |
| ½ | teaspoon vanilla | 2 | mL |
| ⅓ | cup butter, melted, or oil | 75 | mL |
| ¾ | cup sliced almonds | 175 | mL |

**SYRUP**

| | | | |
|---|---|---:|---|
| ⅓ | cup white sugar | 75 | mL |
| 3 | tablespoons water | 45 | mL |
| ¼ | teaspoon almond flavouring or | 1 | mL |
| 1 | tablespoon Amaretto | 15 | mL |

Preheat oven to 350°F (180°C). Sift flour, sugar, baking powder, baking soda and salt. Beat egg. Add buttermilk, vanilla, and butter or oil. Fold into dry ingredients. Batter will be lumpy. Spread in greased 9" (2 L) springform pan. Bake 35 minutes or until lightly browned.

Combine syrup ingredients and boil one minute only. While cake is hot, sprinkle top with almonds and cover with hot almond syrup. Place 6 inches (15 cm) under broiler and brown. Do not leave oven, as it browns quickly.

**Serves 8-10**

**\*TIP:** Leftover buttermilk may be frozen. It does separate but is still suitable for baking.

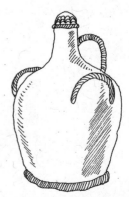

# Apricot Squares

*Very rich and very good!*

| | | | |
|---|---|---|---|
| ⅔ | cup dried apricots | 150 | mL |
| ⅔ | cup water | 150 | mL |
| ½ | cup butter | 125 | mL |
| ¼ | cup sugar | 50 | mL |
| 1 | cup flour | 250 | mL |
| 2 | egg yolks | 2 | |
| ¾ | cup brown sugar | 175 | mL |
| ½ | cup coconut | 125 | mL |
| ½ | cup flour | 125 | mL |
| ¼ | teaspoon salt | 1 | mL |
| ½ | teaspoon baking powder | 2 | mL |

**ICING**

| | | | |
|---|---|---|---|
| ¼ | cup butter | 50 | mL |
| 2 | cups icing sugar | 500 | mL |
| | Rind and juice of 1 lemon | | |

Preheat oven to 300°F (150°C). Cut apricots in small pieces and simmer with the water for 15 minutes or until all of the water is absorbed. Mix butter, sugar and flour and press into a 9" (2.5 L) square cake pan; bake for 15 minutes. Remove from oven and increase oven temperature to 325°F (160°C). Beat 2 eggs yolks and combine with brown sugar, coconut, flour, salt, baking powder, apricots and any remaining cooking water. Spread mixture on crust and bake for 25 minutes. Meanwhile, combine butter, icing sugar and lemon. Spread on cooled squares. Cut into small squares.

**Makes about 25 squares**

# Coconut Almond Cookies

*An elegant cookie!*

| | | | |
|---|---|---|---|
| 1¼ | cups cake and pastry flour | 300 | mL |
| ¼ | teaspoon salt | 1 | mL |
| ½ | cup butter or margarine | 125 | mL |
| ⅓ | cup sugar | 75 | mL |
| 1 | egg yolk | 1 | |
| ½-1 | teaspoon almond extract | 2-5 | mL |
| 1 | egg white, lightly beaten | 1 | |
| 1 | cup coconut, shredded or flaked | 250 | mL |
| ¼ | cup apricot jam | 50 | mL |

Preheat oven to 300°F (150°C). Mix together all ingredients up to and including almond extract. Chill dough for 2 hours before shaping. Roll into 1-inch balls, dip into lightly beaten egg white, then roll in coconut. Place 2 inches (5 cm) apart on greased cookie sheet. With the end of a wooden spoon, make depression in middle of cookie. Bake for 20-25 minutes. Remove to wire rack and fill each cookie with jam.
**Makes 24**

# Pecan Sandies

*Rich and wonderful!*

| | | | |
|---|---|---|---|
| ¾ | cup butter, softened | 175 | mL |
| 3 | tablespoons brown sugar | 45 | mL |
| 1 | cup pecans, chopped | 250 | mL |
| 2 | tablespoons water | 30 | mL |
| 2 | cups cake and pastry flour, sifted | 500 | mL |
| | fruit sugar | | |

Preheat oven to 350°F (180°C). Cream butter; add sugar, flour and water; mix well. Fold in pecans. Roll into balls the size of walnuts. Bake about 15 minutes or until very slightly coloured. Roll in fruit sugar while warm.
**Makes 3 to 4 dozen**

# Chocolate Chip Cheesecake Brownies

*What a wonderful combination of favourite things!*

## CHOCOLATE CHIP BATTER

| | | | |
|---|---|---|---|
| 1 | cup shortening | 250 | mL |
| 1 | cup brown sugar, packed | 250 | mL |
| ½ | cup sugar | 125 | mL |
| 1 | teaspoon vanilla | 5 | mL |
| 3 | eggs | 3 | |
| 2 | cups all-purpose flour, unsifted | 500 | mL |
| 1 | teaspoon baking soda | 5 | mL |
| 1 | teaspoon salt | 5 | mL |
| 1½ | cups chocolate chips (pure & semi-sweet) | 375 | mL |

## CREAM CHEESE BATTER

| | | | |
|---|---|---|---|
| 2 | packages (each 8 oz/250 g) cream cheese, softened | 2 | |
| ¼ | cup sugar | 50 | mL |
| 2 | eggs | 2 | |
| 1 | cup pecans, chopped | 250 | mL |

Preheat oven to 350°F (180°C). Cream shortening, sugars, and vanilla; add eggs and beat well. Combine flour, baking soda and salt. Add to creamed mixture and stir in chocolate chips. Spread one half of the chocolate chip batter in the bottom of a lightly greased 13" × 9" (3.5 L) baking pan. To make the cream cheese batter, combine cheese with sugar and eggs in food processor or mixer and blend until creamy. Pour on top of chocolate chip batter in pan. Sprinkle with nuts. Spread or drop remaining chocolate chip batter by small spoonfuls over cheese filling. Do not be alarmed by tiny sections not filled in by batter—it will spread in the cooking process. Bake in oven for 45 minutes. Cool and cut into pieces.

**Makes about 36 pieces**

# Oatmeal Chocolate Chip Cookies

*Irresistible!*

| | | | |
|---|---|---|---|
| 1 | cup butter | 250 | mL |
| ¾ | cup brown sugar | 175 | mL |
| ¾ | cup white sugar | 175 | mL |
| 2 | eggs | 2 | |
| 1 | teaspoon vanilla | 5 | mL |
| 1½ | cups flour | 375 | mL |
| 1 | teaspoon baking soda | 5 | mL |
| 1 | teaspoon salt | 5 | mL |
| 1 | cup walnuts, chopped | 250 | mL |
| 1 | cup rolled oats | 250 | mL |
| 1½ | cups chocolate chips | 375 | mL |

Preheat oven to 375°F (190°C). Cream butter, brown sugar, white sugar and eggs until light and fluffy. Blend in vanilla. Sift together flour, baking soda and salt. Mix thoroughly with the creamed mixture. Blend in walnuts, rolled oats and chocolate chips. Drop by teaspoonsful onto greased cookie sheet and bake for 10 minutes.
**Makes 5-6 dozen**

# Cookies à la Franks

*Bet you can't eat just one!*

| | | | |
|---|---|---:|---|
| 1 | cup butter | 250 | mL |
| 1 | cup brown sugar | 250 | mL |
| ¼ | cup white sugar | 50 | mL |
| 1 | teaspoon vanilla | 5 | mL |
| 1¼ | cups all-purpose flour, sifted | 300 | mL |
| ½ | cup wheat germ | 125 | mL |
| 1 | teaspoon salt | 5 | mL |
| ½ | teaspoon baking soda | 2 | mL |
| 2 | cups large flake oats | 500 | mL |
| ¼ | cup cold water | 50 | mL |

Preheat oven to 350°F (180°C). Cream butter and sugar together. Add vanilla. Stir in flour, wheat germ, salt, baking soda, oats and water. Drop onto greased baking sheet and press down with fork dipped in cold water. Bake 8-10 minutes.

**Makes 6 dozen**

# Hermits

*An old-time favourite!*

| | | |
|---|---|---|
| 1 | cup butter, softened | 250 mL |
| 1½ | cups brown sugar | 375 mL |
| 3 | eggs, well beaten | 3 |
| 2¾ | cups cake and pastry flour, sifted before measuring | 675 mL |
| ½ | teaspoon baking powder | 2 mL |
| ½ | teaspoon salt | 2 mL |
| ⅓ | teaspoon ground cloves | 2 mL |
| 1 | teaspoon cinnamon | 5 mL |
| ⅓ | teaspoon nutmeg | 2 mL |
| 1 | cup raisins, cut up | 250 mL |
| 1⅓ | cups dates, cut up | 325 mL |
| 1 | cup walnuts, chopped | 250 mL |
| 1 | teaspoon baking soda dissolved in 1 tablespoon (15 mL) hot water | 5 mL |

Preheat oven to 350°F (180°C). Cream the butter and sugar thoroughly. Add the eggs and beat until fluffy. Sift the flour, baking powder, salt and spices together, and stir into the first mixture. Beat well. Add the raisins, dates and nuts. Stir in the baking soda dissolved in hot water. Drop from a teaspoon onto greased cookie sheets and bake for 8-10 minutes. These cookies freeze well.

**Makes 5-6 dozen**

# Sauces and Relishes

# Mrs. Smith's Famous Peach and Pepper Relish

*You can make this all year long and you'll want to!*

| | | | |
|---|---|---|---|
| 5 | hot red peppers | 5 | |
| 12 | sweet red peppers | 12 | |
| 1 | cup wine vinegar | 250 | mL |
| 12 | large peaches, peeled and chopped | 12 | |
| 1 | teaspoon salt | 5 | mL |
| 2 | lemons, cut in half | 2 | |
| 5 | cups sugar | 1.25 | L |

or, if peaches aren't in season ...

| | | | |
|---|---|---|---|
| 5 | hot red peppers | 5 | |
| 10 | sweet red peppers | 10 | |
| 1 | cup wine vinegar | 250 | mL |
| 5 | cans (each 28 oz/796 mL) peaches, chopped and very well drained | 5 | |
| 1 | teaspoon salt | 5 | mL |
| 2 | lemons, cut in half | 2 | |
| 2-3 | cups sugar | 500-750 | mL |

Put peppers in food processor, seeds and all, and process until medium chopped. Add to peaches, vinegar and salt in a large preserving kettle. Add lemon halves. Boil gently for ½ hour. Remove lemons and add sugar. Boil for ½ hour longer or until mixture is thick. Stir frequently to prevent burning. Bottle and seal with paraffin wax. This is excellent served over cream cheese, Brie or Camembert. Also good mixed with cream cheese as a dip for crudités. Wonderful with chicken or pork, too.

**Makes 8-10 jars**

**TIP:** Wilma says a diffuser placed under the pan helps prevent burning.

# Jewel Glaze for Ham

| | | |
|---|---|---|
| 1 | jar (8 oz/250 mL) red currant jelly | 1 |
| ½ | cup golden corn syrup | 125 mL |
| 3 | tablespoons lemon juice | 45 mL |
| 1 | tablespoon vinegar | 15 mL |
| ½ | teaspoon lemon rind, grated | 2 mL |
| ¼ | teaspoon each ground cloves, allspice and cinnamon | 1 mL |
| 1 | cup mixed candied fruit, diced | 250 mL |

Place jelly in a saucepan and mash with fork. Add all ingredients except candied fruit. Bring to a boil over low heat. Stir in candied fruit. Brush on ham or pork roast several times near end of cooking. Try to keep it from dripping into the bottom of the pan as it may burn. Pass remainder at the table as a sauce.

**Makes about 2 cups (500 mL)**

# Jezebel Sauce

*Vary the amount of horseradish to your personal taste and enjoy this unique flavour. Delicious with any meat, hot or cold, and good with cream cheese and crackers too!*

| | | |
|---|---|---|
| 1 | jar (8 oz/250 mL) apple jelly | 1 |
| 1 | jar (8 oz/250 mL) pineapple preserves | 1 |
| ¼-½ | cup moist horseradish | 50-125 mL |
| ½ | teaspoon dry mustard or | 2 mL |
| 1 | tablespoon Dijon mustard | 15 mL |
| | Freshly ground pepper to taste | |

Combine all ingredients and store in the refrigerator. Keeps almost forever!

**Makes about 2½ cups (625 mL)**

# "Our Pesto"

*Delicious spread on pita bread and briefly broiled, or use on pasta—let your imagination go!*

| | | |
|---|---|---|
| 3 | cups washed and dried fresh basil | 750 mL |
| 1 | cup washed and dried fresh spinach | 250 mL |
| 3 | cloves garlic | 3 |
| 2 | tablespoons olive oil (the best you can afford) | 30 mL |
| 1/3 | cup pine nuts | 75 mL |
| 1/2 | cup butter | 125 mL |
| 1/2 | cup freshly grated Parmesan cheese | 125 mL |
| | Freshly ground pepper | |
| | Salt | |

Finely chop basil and spinach in food processor. Add remaining ingredients and blend until smooth. We freeze this in small packages (¼ cup or 50 mL) or in ice cube trays. Thaw and use as desired.

**SOME SERVING SUGGESTIONS:** Put a dollop on any cream soup or tomato soup. Spread some on a steak or stir it into plain white rice. Mix with mayonnaise to make a dip for vegetables or a spread for hamburgers, adult style. Enjoy!

# Green Sauce for Salmon

*Will enhance, not overpower, delicate salmon.*

| | | | |
|---|---|---|---|
| 1 | cup mayonnaise, regular or light | 250 | mL |
| ½ | cup sour cream, regular or light | 125 | mL |
| | Juice of ¼ lemon—more if desired | | |
| ¼ | bunch of watercress, long stems removed | ¼ | |
| 5 | stalks of parsley | 5 | |
| ⅓ | cup chives | 75 | mL |
| 1 | teaspoon marjoram (optional) | 5 | mL |
| 2-3 | sprigs fresh tarragon (optional) | 2-3 | |

Blend all ingredients in food processor. Refrigerate at least 4 hours before serving.

**Makes 2 cups (500 mL)**

# Favourite Mustard Sauce

*Great on a sandwich or as a dip!*

| | | | |
|---|---|---|---|
| ¼ | cup brown sugar | 50 | mL |
| ¼ | cup dry mustard | 50 | mL |
| 3 | eggs, beaten | 3 | |
| ½ | cup white vinegar | 125 | mL |
| ½ | cup 10% cream | 125 | mL |
| | Dash of salt | | |

Combine all ingredients in the top of a double boiler. Cook over hot water, stirring constantly (or almost!), until thickened—about 10 minutes. Cool and keep in refrigerator. This sauce has a wonderfully long storage life.

**Makes 2 cups (500 mL)**

# Extra-Special Hot Barbecue Sauce

*Have water or some other effective cooling agent within reach!*

| | | |
|---|---|---|
| 1 | tablespoon olive oil | 15 mL |
| 1 | medium onion, chopped | 1 |
| 1 | garlic clove, minced | 1 |
| ½ | cup ketchup | 125 mL |
| 2 | tablespoons Worcestershire sauce | 30 mL |
| 1 | cup vinegar | 250 mL |
| 1 | tablespoon sugar | 15 mL |
| 1 | tablespoon dry mustard | 15 mL |
| ½ | tablespoon chili powder | 7.5 mL |
| ½ | tablespoon salt | 7.5 mL |
| | Pepper, paprika (a few shakes of each) | |

Heat a frying pan on medium; when hot, add olive oil. Add onion and garlic. Fry until tan. Add ketchup, Worcestershire and vinegar. Add the rest of the ingredients, stirring thoroughly. Let simmer for ten minutes. Use especially with spareribs. It is also potent with chicken and roast pork.

**Makes about 1½ cups (375 mL)**

# Treats and Treasures

# Butterscotch Sauce

*Good over ice cream or baked Alaska.*

| | | |
|---|---|---|
| 1 | cup white sugar | 250 mL |
| 1 | cup corn syrup | 250 mL |
| ¼ | teaspoon salt | 1 mL |
| 1 | cup whipping cream | 250 mL |
| 1 | teaspoon cornstarch | 5 mL |
| 2 | teaspoons milk | 10 mL |

Cook sugar, syrup, salt and cream together in double boiler for 1 hour. Add cornstarch mixed with milk and cook 3 minutes longer. Serve hot. Keeps indefinitely in refrigerator or freezer.
**Makes 2½-3 cups (625-750 mL)**


# Fudge Sauce

*A thick, wonderful sauce—super simple!*

| | | |
|---|---|---|
| ¼ | cup butter | 50 mL |
| 2 | squares (each 1 oz/28 g) unsweetened chocolate | 2 |
| 1 | cup sugar | 250 mL |
| ½ | cup evaporated milk | 125 mL |

In a double boiler, melt butter and chocolate. Add sugar and mix well. Stir in evaporated milk and cook until sugar is dissolved and sauce is smooth, about 10 minutes. Serve warm over ice cream or anything else that could stand "chocolating up"! Store in refrigerator. Reheat over hot water or in microwave.
**Makes 1 cup (250 mL)**

# Fabulous Sauce for Coffee Ice Cream

*The only thing that improves "Haagen Dazs"!*

| | | | |
|---|---|---|---|
| 1 | cup sugar | 250 | mL |
| 1 | cup water | 250 | mL |
| 1 | teaspoon instant coffee powder | 5 | mL |
| 1 | teaspoon cinnamon | 5 | mL |
| ⅛ | teaspoon ground cloves | 0.5 | mL |
| ⅛ | teaspoon ground nutmeg | 0.5 | mL |
| ¼ | cup coffee-flavoured liqueur | 50 | mL |
| | "Haagen Dazs" coffee ice cream | | |
| | Slivered almonds, toasted or browned in butter | | |

Combine sugar and water in a saucepan. Add coffee powder and spices, stirring over low heat until dissolved. Bring to a boil and boil gently for 10 minutes. Skim off any residue that rises to the surface. Cool. Stir in liqueur. Best if made a couple of days in advance. Will keep for weeks in refrigerator. Sauce will be thin. Serve over coffee ice cream and top with slivered almonds.

**Makes 1½ to 2 cups (375-500 mL)**

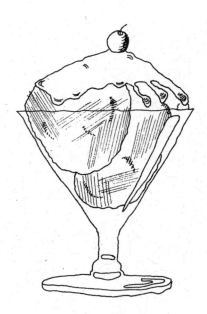

# Caramel Corn

*Kids love it!*

| 7 | quarts popped corn | 7 | L |
|---|---|---|---|
| 2 | cups brown sugar | 500 | mL |
| 1 | cup butter | 250 | mL |
| ½ | cup corn syrup | 125 | mL |
| 1 | teaspoon salt | 5 | mL |
| ½ | teaspoon baking soda | 2 | mL |
| 1 | teaspoon vanilla | 5 | mL |

Preheat oven to 250°F (120°C). Boil sugar, butter, syrup and salt together for 5 minutes. Remove from heat; add baking soda and vanilla. Mix well and pour over popped corn. Toss until well coated. Place in a large roasting pan or on cookie sheets and bake for 1 hour, stirring every 15 minutes. When cooled, store in closed containers. Add mixed nuts for a special treat.

# Chocolate Caramels

*Definitely a yummy caramel!*

| | | | |
|---|---|---|---|
| 2 | cups white sugar | 500 | mL |
| 2 | cups 10% cream | 500 | mL |
| 1 | cup corn syrup | 250 | mL |
| ½ | teaspoon salt | 2 | mL |
| 2 | squares (each 1 oz/28 g) unsweetened chocolate | 2 | |
| ⅓ | cup butter | 75 | mL |
| 1 | teaspoon vanilla | 5 | mL |

In a large saucepan, mix sugar, 1 cup (250 mL) cream, syrup, salt and chocolate. Bring to a boil over medium heat, stirring constantly. Gradually add remaining cream, making sure that the mixture does not stop boiling. Boil for another 5 minutes without stirring. Stir in butter and cook, stirring constantly, until mixture reaches 248°F (120°C) on a candy thermometer (firm ball stage). Remove from heat and stir in vanilla. Pour into a greased 8" (2 L) square pan. Cool and cut into pieces. If desired, wrap in squares of wax paper.
**Makes 64 tiny pieces**

# Swedish Nuts

*A good Christmas treat!*

| | | |
|---|---|---|
| 1½ | cups blanched almonds | 375 mL |
| 2 | cups walnut or pecan halves or a combination of each | 500 mL |
| 2 | egg whites | 2 |
| 1 | cup white sugar | 250 mL |
| | Pinch of salt | |
| ½ | cup butter | 125 mL |

Preheat oven to 325°F (160°C). Toast nuts in slow oven until light brown. Beat egg whites until soft peaks form. Fold in sugar and salt. Fold nuts into egg whites. Melt butter in a 15" × 10" (2 L) jelly roll pan. Spread nut mixture over butter. Bake slowly for 30 minutes stirring with a spatula every 10 minutes or until nuts are coated with a brown covering and no butter remains in the pan. Cool, separate nuts, then store covered in a cool place or refrigerator.

**Makes 4 cups (1 L)**

# Chocolate-Covered Strawberries

*A special yet simple ending for any meal!*

| | | |
|---|---|---|
| 15-20 | strawberries | 15-20 |
| 6 | squares (each 1 oz/28 g) semi-sweet or white Swiss chocolate | 6 |

Wash and dry berries but do not hull. Melt chocolate over hot water. Dip berries in the chocolate one at a time and let excess drip off. Place on a wax paper–lined cookie sheet and refrigerate until firm, or overnight. Arrange on a plate or serve in candy wrappers.
**Makes 15-20**

# Chocolate-Covered Leaves

| | | |
|---|---|---|
| | Leaves—rose, camellia or any attractive non-toxic leaves | |
| 4 | squares (each 1 oz/28 g) semi-sweet chocolate | 4 |

Wash and dry leaves. Melt chocolate in the top of a double boiler. Line a baking sheet with wax paper. With a table knife, spread melted chocolate on undersides of leaves. Place leaves, chocolate side up, on baking sheet and refrigerate or freeze. To serve, remove leaf by gently grasping stem and pulling chocolate off. Discard real leaves and use chocolate leaves to decorate a special dessert.

# Turtles

| 1 | can (12 oz/300 mL) Eagle brand condensed milk (not low fat) | 1 |
| ½ | pound pecan halves | 250 g |
| 2 | German or Swiss chocolate bars (each 4 oz/113 g) | 2 |

To make caramel, pour condensed milk in top of a double boiler; cover. Place over boiling water. Over low heat, simmer 1-1½ hours or until thick and light caramel-coloured. Stir vigorously until smooth. Cool. Cover and refrigerate overnight. This will keep in the refrigerator for weeks. Make small balls of caramel and place on greased cookie sheet. Place 5 pecan halves in each ball to simulate a turtle. Melt chocolate and spoon 1 teaspoon (5 mL) over each turtle. Cool. Do not refrigerate.

# Lease-Breaking Egg Nog

| 12 | egg yolks | 12 |
| 1 | pound fruit sugar | 500 g |
| 1 | quart Barbados rum | 1 L |
| 1 | quart whole milk | 1 L |
| 2 | cups whipping cream, whipped nutmeg | 500 mL |

Combine the first four ingredients and allow to rest 3-4 hours or overnight in refrigerator. Just before serving, fold in the whipped cream. Top with nutmeg.

**Makes 3 quarts (3 L)**

# Café Brûlot

| | | |
|---|---|---|
| | **Peel of an orange cut in one continuous strip** | |
| | **Whole cloves** | |
| 1 | **3-inch (7.5-cm) piece of cinnamon** | 1 |
| 1 | **piece lemon peel, 3 inches (7.5 cm) long** | 1 |
| 6 | **lumps sugar** | 6 |
| 1 | **cup brandy** | 250 mL |
| ¼ | **cup Cointreau** | 50 mL |
| 1 | **teaspoon vanilla** | 5 mL |
| 1 | **quart strong, black coffee** | 1 L |

Stud the orange peel at 1-inch (2.5-cm) intervals with cloves. Combine with cinnamon, lemon peel and sugar in a heat-proof punch bowl. At serving time, heat brandy. Add Cointreau and vanilla to ingredients in bowl. Pour in hot coffee. Add brandy, reserving 1 ladleful. Ignite remaining brandy, pour over coffee in bowl and bring to table while still flaming.

**Serves 4**

# Candied Grapes

| 1   | egg white                    | 1      |
| --- | ---------------------------- | ------ |
| ½   | cup sugar                    | 125 mL |
| 1   | teaspoon cinnamon            | 5 mL   |
| ½   | teaspoon ground cardamom     | 2 mL   |
|     | Green or red grapes          |        |

Beat egg white until frothy. Mix sugar, cinnamon and cardamom together. Cut grapes into small clusters. Dip first in the egg white. Shake off excess. Roll grapes in sugar mixture. Refrigerate on a rack until coating is set or overnight.

# Apricots in Cognac

*Serve with cheese in lieu of dessert!*

| 1   | pound dried apricots      | 500 g |
| --- | ------------------------- | ----- |
|     | Cognac or gin to cover    |       |

Let stand, covered, at least 24 hours. The flavour reaches its peak if allowed to stand for 1 week.
**Serves 6-8**

# Index